THE HIDDEN HAND OF GOD

MIRACULOUS HEALINGS

THE HIDDEN HAND OF GOD

MIRACULOUS HEALINGS

Surely there are in everyone's life certain connections, twists and turns which pass awhile under the category of Chance, but at the last, well examined, prove to be the very hand of God.

—Sir Thomas Browne

Guideposts®

CARMEL • NEW YORK 10512

www.guideposts.org

Acknowledgments

Every attempt has been made to credit the sources of copyrighted material used in this book. If any such acknowledgment has been inadvertently omitted or miscredited, receipt of such information would be appreciated.

Scripture marked (KJV) are taken from *The New Open Bible, Study Edition*, King James Version. Copyright © 1990 by Thomas Nelson, Inc.

Scripture marked (NIV) are taken from *The Holy Bible, New International Version.* Copyright © 1973, 1978, 1984 International Bible Society. Used by permission of Zondervan Bible Publishers.

Scripture marked (NKJV) are taken from *The Holy Bible*, New King James Version. Copyright © 1997, 1990, 1985, 1983 by Thomas Nelson, Inc.

Scripture marked (NRSV) are taken from the *Common Bible*, New Revised Standard Version Bible. Copyright © 1989 by the Division of Christian Education of the National Council of the Churches of Christ in the U.S.A. Used by permission. All rights reserved.

"A Perfect Child" by Kathleen Lukens originally appeared in *Guideposts* magazine (February 1994). Copyright © 1993 by Guideposts, Carmel, NY 10512. All rights reserved.

"Angel in a Different Pew" by Eva Unga is reprinted by permission of the author. Copyright © 1999 by Eva Unga.

"Because He Is Good" by Rebekah Montgomery is published in *Ordinary Miracles* copyright © 2000. Published by Promise Press, an imprint of Barbour Publishing, Inc., PO Box 719, Uhrichsville, Ohio 44683.

"Christ's Healing Power" by Marie Clowdis-Coon is reprinted by permission of the author. Copyright © 1999 by Marie Clowdis-Coon.

"Covered with the Word" by Linda Shublak originally appeared in *Guideposts* magazine (September 1996). Copyright © 1996 by Guideposts, Carmel, NY 10512. All rights reserved.

"Crash!" by Jeremy V. Jones. *Breakaway* magazine, 2000, Vol. 11, No. 6, published by Focus on the Family. Copyright © 2000, Focus on the Family. All rights reserved. International copyright secured. Used by permission.

"The Divine Touch" by Mark Buntain is published in *I Saw the Lord* by Chester and Lucille Huyssen. Copyright © 1977, 1992 by Chester Huyssen. Published by Chosen Books, a division of Baker Book House.

"Erin's Christmas Vision" by Joan Wester Anderson is from *Where Wonders Prevail.* Copyright © 1996 by Joan Wester Anderson. Reprinted by permission of Ballantine Books, a division of Random House Inc.

"Expect a Miracle" by Dawn Stobbe, as told to Meg Lundstrom. Reprinted by permission of Dawn Stobbe and Meg Lundstrom. Copyright © 1996 by Dawn Stobbe and Meg Lundstrom.

(continued on page 167)

THE HIDDEN HAND OF GOD

MIRACULOUS HEALINGS

Introduction. . . vii

W hen most of us think of healing, we think of our physical needs: diseases like cancer, stroke and heart disease, or injuries from auto accidents, near-drownings and assaults. But in our most private moments, we recognize that our brokenness is much more complicated. Our lives are littered with broken relationships, careers, dreams, even our faith. Every area of our lives bears scars of our wounds, injuries inflicted both by neglect and by design. While some of these injuries appear benign and unimportant, most of us will admit, when pressed, that for most of us it is our injuries that define our lives.

This brokenness can reach the point where we consider it simply "normal." Dishonesty, neglect, anger, discouragement and maliciousness, as well as addictions of every variety—all become routine parts of our lives, creating wounds in ourselves and others every bit as damaging as an injury from an auto accident. This broken-ness ultimately affects our most fundamental relationship, our relationship to our Creator.

The only solution for the broken places in our lives is healing. At first glance, this seems an odd term to apply to all these situations in our lives. It's one thing to talk about healing for physical problems. After all, seeking healing for a sick child or blind spouse is as natural as breathing. We see a need, we acknowledge God's power to meet that need, and we ask for His intervention to make something that is broken whole again.

But healing is also what is needed in all areas of our lives. Our relationships need God's touch to restore them and make them whole, and our daily lives need God's touch to transform all those destructive elements of our lives that so easily become part of us.

It is this need for complete healing that Jesus emphasized. When we read the stories of Jesus healing people, we see several things. Jesus obviously has the power to heal people of their physical diseases and injuries, and He generously uses His gift to bring relief to people. But what is also apparent is that Jesus always expresses concern because people don't realize that another healing, a deeper healing, is available simply for the asking.

The stories in *Miraculous Healings* are mostly about people who have experienced physical healing; they are faced with severe injuries and disabling diseases, and finally cry out to God for healing. These stories excite us and encourage us to remember God's faithfulness and to praise His goodness. But included here also are stories of God's healing in other ways: a mother's heart, a husband's faith, a carpenter's new skill.

A *New Yorker* cartoon shows a woman speaking to her doctor: "Please, doc—nothing too aggressive. I'm kind of attached to my symptoms." As we read these stories, may we not be so attached to our symptoms that we cannot find the healing we need in our lives.

Chapter 1 Lord, Heal My Child!

While he was saying this, a ruler came and knelt before him and said, "My daughter has just died. But come and put your hand on her, and she will live." Jesus got up and went with him, and so did his disciples.

When Jesus entered the ruler's house and saw the flute players and the noisy crowd, he said, "Go away. The girl is not dead but asleep." But they laughed at him. After the crowd had been put outside, he went in and took the girl by the hand, and she got up. News of this spread through all that region (Matthew 9:18-19, 23-26, NIV; see also Mark 5:22-24, 35-43, NIV; Luke 8:41-42, 49-56, NIV).

A grandmother relates a story about her son, the young father of a two-year-old named Philip, who was tripping and stumbling his way through the toddler years. Philip's first fall of the day was met with considerable tears and frustration that required a long period of consoling on Daddy's part. After things had finally returned to normal, Daddy reached for his cordless phone to make a call, only to watch Philip tumble forward once again, reinjuring himself and filling the air with wails of pain. Filled with anger and frustration, Dad slammed the phone onto the sidewalk, shattering it completely, and scooped up his son to comfort him. "I was so mad that my son got hurt that I just couldn't take it!" he later told his mother. "How can God let a little boy get hurt?"

For most of us, there is a particular poignancy about a child who is facing an illness or injury. We feel as that young father did: How can God allow a child to hurt? And though we may not, for whatever reasons, seek God's intervention for our own healing, we will not hesitate to ask God to heal a child.

Stories in which healing comes to a child appeal to us not only because they affirm God's love for us, but also because they reaffirm our hopes for the future. Children allow us to reach into the future, and when their lives are whole and healthy, our fundamental hopes for the future are secure.

The parents in these stories each reached out to God, asking for healing for their children. Sometime the healing was quick, sometimes it took place over time. But in every case, our loving God provided healing—both to child and to parent.

As a father has compassion on his children,
so the LORD has compassion on those who fear him;
* for he knows how we are formed,*
* he remembers that we are dust.*

—Psalm 103:13, 14 (NIV)

MARTY'S MIRACLE GIFT EXCHANGE

KELSEY TYLER

Diane Rayner always cherished the wonder of Christmas and the magical feelings of joy that went with the holiday season. She pondered frequently the first Christmas two thousand years ago, when on a clear night a new and brilliant star shining over Bethlehem announced the miracle of God's son coming to earth as a child. It seemed that no matter how crimped the family budget was, the Christmas holidays were always rich in spirit for the Rayners.

Especially that Christmas when Diane's youngest child, Marty, was eight years old.

Marty was a blond, brown-eyed boy whose smile could light a room. Because of a prolonged illness years earlier, he was deaf in his left ear and had a habit of cocking his head to one side so he could hear better when someone spoke to him. It was a deafness doctors claimed they were unable to repair.

That year, Diane and her children had just moved into a mobile home in a forested area outside Redmond, Washington. The typical rainy winter season seemed never to let up. Dark gray skies perpetually pounded the muddy ground with a chilling downpour.

But inside the small trailer, the Rayners shared a gleeful anticipation as Christmas neared. Still, no one was happier than Marty. He had a new best friend named Kenny and for the past few months the two boys had been inseparable. The rainy Pacific Northwest weather was never a deterrent for the young boys.

Their world of adventure was in the wooded horse pasture bordering both their homes. The pasture also had a beautiful meadow with a stream running through it, a magnificent playground, a dream come true for the adventurous twosome.

They would play for hours in the woods and meadow, searching for frogs and grass snakes along the stream. Sometimes they would dangle carrots for the horses or hang suet balls coated with seeds for the birds. Once in a while they would offer a spoonful of peanut butter to a perplexed squirrel. Other times they would remodel their scrap-wood fort, searching forgotten treasure and acting out a multitude of imaginary scenarios.

The pasture that bordered their homes was protected by an electric fence, and shortly after Marty moved in, both boys became adept at slithering under the lowest hot wire to avoid what could be a serious electrical shock.

As Christmas drew closer, Diane realized that Marty was acting secretive, hiding away the few pennies he earned for allowance and taking special care to make his bed and take out the trash. He even helped his older siblings set the table at night so they were ready to eat dinner as soon as their mom got home from work.

"What are you up to, anyway?" Diane would ask, sweeping the boy into a hug.

Marty would shrug, his big brown eyes dancing with excitement. "It's a Christmas surprise, Mom." And then he would hurry off to complete another chore.

Pinching pennies was sometimes quite a challenge for this family of four, but Diane, a working single parent, taught her children to be creative, using their imagination and inexpensive household items to decorate their home for Christmas. There were woven paper ornaments on the tree and handmade gifts underneath. Diane tried to make her children feel as if they had been blessed with abundance. In her words, the Lord had provided them with elegance on a shoestring.

Many times Kenny joined in the cookie baking, craft projects, and decorating, working alongside the Rayners at their small kitchen table. But then the boys would have an idea and instantly they would be out the door, sliding cautiously under the electric fence and playing once more in the fields. Then, in an hour or so they would be back at Diane's table, helping make paper creations or stringing popcorn for the tree.

"Remember," Diane would tell her children on those cold, rainy afternoons, "Christmas is a celebration of the Christ child's birthday. It isn't about receiving a lot of toys and gifts for yourself. It's about giving treasure, gifts of love, to others. That's what God did when He sent His baby son to us that very first Christmas."

Diane was jubilant at the thought of Marty's special gift. Her youngest child seemed to understand the Christmas message better than anyone, and as December wore on he worked and saved like never before.

As financially difficult as things were for the Rayners, Diane knew that Kenny's family was struggling even harder to make ends meet.

Even little Marty could see how Kenny's family scrimped to survive month to month on their meager income. As Christmas neared, Diane suspected her son was saving money to buy something extra special for Kenny's Christmas.

Less than a week before Christmas, Diane was making Danish cinnamon cookies one night when Marty approached her, his eyes filled with pride.

"Mom, I bought Kenny a Christmas present," he said, bursting with excitement. "Wanna see it?"

Diane pulled her hands out of the dough she'd been kneading and washed them in the sink. "Of course I do," she said. Then she dried her hands carefully on a towel.

"Let's see what you have there, little guy."

Marty smiled and his enthusiasm was contagious. "Well, it's something he's wanted for a long time, Mom," the boy said.

He carefully pulled a small box from his pocket and lifted the lid. Diane peered inside and saw a small plastic pocket compass, the treasure Marty had spent weeks saving for.

"It's a wonderful Christmas gift," Diane said and she smiled at Marty. But even as she did, her heart filled with doubts. Kenny's mother was an admirable and fiercely proud lady, and though they were barely surviving, she would refuse any offer of charity. It was doubtful that Kenny's family could afford to exchange gifts among themselves, and Diane knew there was no way they could purchase presents for people outside the family.

Diane realized she had to explain the situation to Marty. She told him that although his gift would come with the best intentions, Kenny's mother might not let him accept it.

Marty grinned. "I know, Mom," he said. "But it's going to be a secret. They'll never, ever know who it's from. It'll stay a mystery."

Diane studied the child before her and smiled with pride. Not only had he saved his allowance and purchased a gift for his friend, he had already devised a way to make it a secret so Kenny's family wouldn't feel awkward.

This is truly the spirit of giving, Diane thought. This is what Christmas is all about.

Christmas Eve finally arrived along with cold, continuous rain and dreary skies. Inside the Rayners' small trailer home, Diane and her three children bustled about making sure every gift was wrapped perfectly and carefully placed under the tree.

Friends and family were planning to drop by the next day to celebrate the Christ child's birthday, and Diane busied herself with final preparations.

As darkness fell over the Pacific Northwest, Diane worked in her kitchen and stared out the window at the dismal rain. Somehow it didn't seem right that Christmas Eve would have the same gloomy bone-chilling rain as any other winter night.

Where is the mystery, the magic, the miracle, God? she wondered silently.

Because of the heavy cloud cover there wasn't a single star in the sky and Diane wondered how anything strange and wonderful could happen on such a miserable night. Certainly this soggy evening could not compare with the clear and star-filled night when a miracle happened and the Christ child came to earth many centuries ago.

Diane sighed and crossed the tiny kitchen to check on the ham and bread in the oven. As she did, she saw Marty walk quietly toward the coat closet and slip his coat over his flannel pajamas. In his hand he clutched the small, brightly wrapped gift for Kenny.

"Be right back, Mom," he whispered. The little boy sounded so serious, about to undertake his secret mission. But there was a twinkle in his eyes that lifted Diane's spirits. Just how proud could a mother be? she wondered.

"Be very, very careful." She wiped her hands on her apron and watched her son disappear through the front door.

Through the rain-drenched wooded pasture Marty ran, traveling as quickly as his short little legs would carry him. He slid carefully under the electric fence and sped all the way to Kenny's house. Quietly he moved up the steps, placing the gift just inside the screen door. His heart raced with anticipation as he rang the doorbell.

Then in a flash, Marty flew down the steps and back into the rainy, dark night, running as fast as he could. He had to get away so that Kenny's family wouldn't see him.

But in his hasty exit he forgot about the electric fence.

Without warning, Marty suddenly crashed against it and was immediately thrown onto the wet ground, his small body reeling from the painful electric shock. For several minutes Marty lay on the ground, tingling and trying to catch his breath. Then he forced himself to his feet, felt his left cheek and winced. The hot wire had snagged him under his ear and that side of his face was burning with pain.

He was unsteady as he made his way back to the trailer. Rain soaked through his coat into his pajamas and he was drenched by the time he stumbled inside. Diane gasped when she saw him and rushed to his side.

"Marty, what happened to you?" she knelt beside him, wrapping her arms around his muddy body.

"The fence," Marty cried. "I forgot about the electric fence."

Diane felt sick. She pictured her generous little son jolted to the ground in the moments after delivering such a special gift. She could see that Marty was still dazed from the shock and she carefully examined the burn mark, a red line developing along the left side of his face from his mouth to his ear.

After tending the burn, Diane drew him a warm, soothing bath, made him a hot cup of cocoa, and within a short time, wearing fresh, dry pajamas, he was feeling much better. Just before Diane tucked him into bed, Marty remembered Kenny's gift.

"Know what?" he whispered.

"What?" Diane reached for the boy's hand and held it gently in her own. She was disappointed that the boy's gift-giving had turned into such a painful event. Especially on Christmas Eve.

Marty smiled then and Diane could see he'd forgotten about the burn. "He didn't see who delivered the gift, Mom. I'm sure he doesn't know it's from me."

Diane smiled sadly. "You are a very special and kind person, Marty. Your mom is extremely proud of you."

But hours later, Diane was still depressed about the incident. Marty had saved for months for that gift and had taken it to Kenny with all the love a young boy could muster. In return he was badly shocked, thrown to the muddy, wet ground, and his face was branded with a sore, ugly red burn blister.

Diane wrestled with her thoughts. *He was doing what You want, Lord,* she prayed silently. *But what happened tonight makes this Christmas Eve far worse than any night we've had all year. No wonderful miracles or mysterious awesome wonders. Just misery for a little boy. It doesn't seem fair, Lord.*

The next morning, Christmas Day dawned sunny and warm. The rain had finally stopped, and after days of cold, gloomy weather, sunshine filled the skies. The children awoke joyously, unaware of Diane's disappointment the night before.

"It doesn't really hurt too bad, Mom," Marry said and hugged his mother, smiled up at her. She looked at the burn on his face and saw that although it was still ugly, red, and badly blistered, it was not infected. She hoped it would not leave a scar.

She counted her blessings, said a silent prayer of thanks, and figured it was a small miracle in and of itself that the little fellow wasn't more seriously injured, receiving an electrical impact like that in the rain. Then she relaxed and allowed herself to be caught up in the children's enthusiasm.

During the bright morning the Rayner family opened their presents, and as they did, Kenny rang the doorbell.

"Look at this!" he said in awe. "You won't believe it, Marry, someone came and left a gift on our porch last night. I got a new compass!"

Diane and Marty exchanged a quick grin. Kenny obviously did not know who the gift was from and had not seen Marty leaving his house the night before. The two boys admired the compass and began talking about the adventures to come now that they had a new way of navigating their cherished meadow and woods.

As the boys talked, Diane noticed something strange. She watched her son carefully, studying him and trying to understand what was happening. Marty was not cocking his head when he listened to his friend. He actually seemed to be understanding Kenny with his deaf ear.

"Marty," Diane said and approached him, puzzled. "Does your hearing sound different?"

Marty shrugged. "I think so," he said. "Things seem louder than before and I don't have to work so hard to hear when people are talking to me."

Diane performed some preliminary hearing tests, and each time it seemed that Marty's left ear, the one that had been deaf since he was a toddler, was working now. When Marty was back at school following the holidays, the school nurse ran another check on his hearing. A report came home declaring that the hearing in Marty's left ear was completely normal.

Diane reflected on that memorable Christmas Eve, about the special gift and the electric shock Marty received as he ran back home that night.

"God, in all His mercy, saw a little boy whose gift came from the heart," Diane would say later. "In return, Marty's left ear, medically unfixable, was healed. That was a miracle only God could perform."

Later doctors confirmed the nurse's test results and suggested that the electric shock Marty received from the fence was somehow responsible for reconnecting damaged nerve impulses and restoring the boy's hearing.

Diane and Marty understood the incident as a true blessing. It had happened, after all, on Christmas Eve—the night when strange and miraculous things still happen to those who believe that with God all things are possible.

THE GIFT OF HOPE

SURIE FETTMAN

We didn't get to hear our oldest son's first cry, but the obstetrician later told us that it was actually a strangled scream. On February 11, 1989, our son was delivered by emergency C-section due to fetal distress. I was under general anesthesia, and my husband was waiting anxiously outside the operating room.

My baby's lungs were full of meconium—that first sticky, dark green bowel movement that is usually released by infants shortly after birth. But fetal distress caused our son to release it while still in my uterus, and it polluted the previously sterile amniotic fluid. The meconium became embedded in our tiny son's lungs.

I came out of an anesthetic stupor and looked around. The operating room was quiet and empty, except for a lone nurse fiddling with a surgical tray. There was a dull ache in my abdomen, and I felt dizzy. My husband was standing at the door to the OR. He moved close to me when he saw I was awake.

"What did we have?" I asked weakly.

"A little boy," my husband said. He seemed subdued.

"I'm so sorry it didn't work out like we planned," I ventured, referring to the C-section.

"It doesn't matter," my husband assured me. "What matters now is that our son needs to recover. He is very sick. He was rushed into the neonatal intensive care unit."

"Oh, God!" I cried. As my husband continued to explain the circumstances to me, I pleaded, over and over, "Oh, God, please save my baby."

Because I developed a fever after the surgery, it was more than a day later when I finally got to see my baby. He lay still and sedated on an open warming table, his fragile newborn body invaded by tubes and needles. He was beautiful. A dark black fuzz of hair framed his round face, and long dark lashes brushed his pale cheeks.

My husband stood near me as tears rolled down my cheeks, and I sang a lullaby softly to my son. I talked to him and I prayed. I was so young, only nineteen, and with all my heart and soul, I wanted my baby to live.

But the neonatologist told us that the prognosis was very poor. There had been absolutely no change in the baby's condition since he was born. He was alive only because of the respirator and the other life-giving equipment that surrounded his tiny body. And when our pediatrician heard that I was pumping and storing milk, she told my family to talk to me about it.

"Somebody has to prepare her. That baby is probably not going to make it." Nobody had the heart to give me her message. But I was not naive. I knew how seriously my son's condition was; I just refused to give up hope. Five times a day I sat down with my breast pump, and as I pumped the milk I bargained with God.

"God, I'm doing what I can for this baby. Now You do Your part."

When our son was nine days old my husband and I came into the NICU for our daily visit.

"Oh, no!" I said to the nurse. "What's the matter with him?" The baby was gray, and his body looked as shriveled as an old man's. The nurse didn't answer, but she offered to wrap him up so we could hold him. We knew this meant the end was near. Until then we had not been allowed even to touch him.

She wrapped the baby up, wires and all, in a soft cotton blanket and placed him in my arms. He felt light as a feather. My husband leaned over my shoulder to get closer to his son. The nurse used a Polaroid camera to take our first family picture. As my husband and I held him we talked to him, and begged him to live.

"I want you to much, Little Lamb," I said.

That night I sang to my son and kissed him good night. We tore ourselves away from him and went home. When I arrived at the NICU the next morning, the nurses grabbed me and hugged me, and actually danced me to my son's crib. He was awake, his cheeks looked filled out, and they were pink. He looked up at me with the dark eyes I had never yet seen.

"It's a miracle," we were told. "During the night your son's vital signs picked up dramatically and he even started trying to breathe on his own. We were able to turn the respirator down from a hundred percent to sixty percent."

But he wasn't happy. He struggled against the respirator, turning his little head back and forth, trying to free himself from the pipe sticking down his throat. His mouth opened in soundless wails. My heart wrenched for him, but as soon as I held his hand and started singing to him, he calmed down. He looked up at me and blinked his eyes, and soon he fell back to sleep.

Convinced that my baby responded so favorably to the voice he had come to know over the last nine months, the nurses suggested that I sing into a little cassette recorder so they could turn it on for him when I wasn't in the unit. We bought a minirecorder and I sang lullabies and soothing folk songs until I had filled up an entire tape. I sang every song I knew—all the tunes I had been humming to myself throughout my pregnancy. The nurses told me that every time they turned on the recorder, the baby would calm down and cease his struggling. It was reassuring to know that I made such a difference in my son's well-being. I had felt so helpless until then. But now I felt useful and necessary. Even though my son was still ill, we were filled with joy. He was going to make it. As he turned two weeks old, he was finally removed from the respirator.

We were now able to share in his care. We diapered him, sponged him, and took turns holding him. And the milk I had expressed for him was administered through a feeding tube. I felt jubilant that I could finally care for my son.

At three weeks he graduated to getting my milk from a bottle. When I fed him the first time he gulped the milk down with gusto and then let the nipple slide from his mouth. He looked straight into my eyes and smiled.

When he was four weeks old I was able to breast-feed him. The nurses warned me that it would probably be a struggle. Many babies develop nipple confusion if they are not breast-fed soon after birth. But my baby latched right on and cuddled into my breast. He started gaining his weight back, and he was soon transferred to the nursery. A week later we brought him home, completely healthy and back to his birth weight of six pounds, twelve ounces.

Although the first month of my son's life was precarious, I never gave up hope. Hope was the one ray of sunshine in the dark shadows of my life. I knew that when hope was gone, so too was the life force. And if hope was kept alive, so too was our determination to go on.

The whole family joined us in celebrating his circumcision, his *bris*, when he was officially named. He was named after my grandfather, Nathaniel, and we all thought it was so appropriate. Nathaniel means "a gift from God." And our son is a very precious gift indeed.

CHRIST'S HEALING POWER

MARIE CLOWDIS-COON

t was an unusually balmy, springlike day for the last week of March 1968. Our family had recently moved into our "new" one hundred-year-old home in Oakville. Winter had held us captive in the house long enough. Tanya, age seventeen months, Jay, age three and a half, and I had spent all day in the yard. They had played while I raked and removed the debris that had collected during the fall and winter months.

The arrival of the school bus and our other two children, eight-year-old Cindy and six-and-a-half-year-old Robin, alerted me to the fact that I'd become so absorbed in the yard work that I'd neglected to start dinner on time. Oh well, hot dogs were quick and one of the kids' favorite meals.

While waiting for the hot dogs to come to a boil, I went into the living room to talk to my husband, Gorden. He had just come home from work at the Farmer's Elevator. In a matter of minutes, our quiet conversation about the day's events was broken by screams from our four children in the kitchen.

Tanya, hungry from playing outside in the fresh air, had grown impatient and decided to help herself to the hot dogs, which by then had come to a rapid boil. The pan of scalding water had emptied itself on her face, neck and chest.

Cindy was already pulling off the white sweater Tanya wore when Gorden came through the doorway. He yanked off her corduroy shirt so quickly that buttons flew across the room. Next came the little white tee shirt, also wet and steaming.

Hearing the commotion, a neighbor from across the street came through our front door as we were wrapping Tanya in a clean sheet. I sat rocking our crying baby back and forth on my lap, trying to soothe away the pain. While assuring me that everything would be all right, the friend removed the curlers that I'd placed in my hair earlier. Her husband, a county policeman, arrived home as we were going out the door; he whisked us into his car. Within minutes, we were at the hospital.

The emergency room doctor and nurses seemed cool and brusque. Perhaps the sight of Gorden in his dusty work clothes and me in my soiled jeans, flannel shirt and rumpled hair gave them the wrong impression. The expression of "negligent parents" written on their faces and in their tone of voice made my already unbearable guilt even heavier.

When I heard the doctor instruct the nurses to admit our crying baby, my heart sank. I had prayed they would treat her and then we'd all be on our way home. The doctor's caustic parting words rang in my ears: " . . . if she lives." There had been no doubt in my mind that it was a serious injury, but the idea that it might be life-threatening never occurred to me until that moment.

They moved Tanya into a room, and then the charge nurse informed me that I would not be permitted to stay with her. The thought that I was expected simply to walk away from my baby's side, believing she might die during the night, was almost more than I could handle.

While Gorden returned home to comfort the other children, I stood in Tanya's room, crying and praying that God wouldn't let our precious baby die. As I did so, some men appeared at the doorway.

Since we had not yet become regulars at the Oakville Brethren Church, it's not surprising that I barely recognized the men in the doorway as being from the church. They were trying to convince the nurse to let them enter Tanya's room. This nurse, who resembled a Marine Corps drill sergeant, asked if one of these men was my minister. Eagerly, I answered, "Yes!"

Begrudgingly, she admitted them, adding curtly that they had "only a few minutes!"

I saw three men enter the dimly lit room and stand across from me beside Tanya's bed. I can't remember what was said, only that they—and I silently with them— prayed that God would heal this child. Then, all too quickly, they were gone.

My pleas to stay with Tanya were to no avail. A uniformed security guard escorted me to the lobby. The twenty-minute drive through the dark countryside seemed to take an eternity as I traveled home, continuing to plead with God to watch over Tanya and to forgive me for allowing such a terrible thing to happen to her.

At eight o'clock the next morning, I could hardly believe my eyes as I entered Tanya's room. The third-degree burns on her face were gone! Not one trace of the blazing red skin, so prominent just hours earlier, remained. Only clear, soft, white skin. Her neck and shoulder were the only areas that bore the scars of that boiling water. She was not only alive, but healed.

It wasn't until after Tanya's release from the hospital that we learned the identity of the men who had prayed over Tanya that first night. They were Deacon Richard Smith and Deacon Jerry Covington.

"But who was the third man?" I asked.

"What third man?" they replied.

"There were *three* men. I saw them," I said.

Dick smiled. "Yes, I believe you did."

Do you suppose? Was it really *Him*?

WHILE MY PARENTS SLEPT

EMMA WILFORD

Religious faith may seem elusive to some people in our modern age, but for me it's never been a problem. It's not just because I was raised by devout Italian immigrants. More important was something I witnessed as a seven-year-old girl living in Cleveland. Ever since that June afternoon more than seventy-five years ago, faith in God's power has been as natural to me as breathing.

I was the fifth of six children born to Paulo Florio and Assunta Ciccarelli, who lived in a wooden frame house on West Sixtieth Street, in a sprawling, ethnically mixed neighborhood. Their first child, Dominick, was born in 1904, soon followed by Mary, Rose, Theresa, me and little Anthony. Papa worked long hours with the Cleveland Railway Company to support us, and wasn't home much. Momma was busy doing laundry, mending clothes, shopping and cooking—yet I never heard her once complain. She had strong religious faith and took us all to church every Sunday.

My brothers, sisters and I all looked up to Dom, our big brother. Tall and handsome, Dom had straight black hair parted stylishly down the middle. With large, expressive brown eyes and a beguiling smile, he charmed everyone he met. Never drawn to book-learning, Dom quit school after the eighth grade to make money to help us all out. He worked as a shoe salesman, and bought us treats with his weekly salary. Robust and confident, he had never been sick a day in his life. Momma and Papa doted on him, as we all did.

Then, one morning late in the spring of 1920, when Dom was seventeen, he didn't appear for breakfast. "Where's Dominick?" Momma asked, dishing out our oatmeal.

I put down my spoon and dashed upstairs, peeking around his door. He lay in bed.

"Dom?" I said. He waved at me feebly. "I'm too tired to get up," he said. Momma appeared and put her hand on his forehead. "He has a fever," she said. She brought cold cloths for his head.

But hour by hour the fever got higher. After two days he became delirious. Thank goodness Papa was home, and he and Momma managed to get Dom to nearby St. John Hospital.

The diagnosis was grim: "Brain fever"—spinal meningitis. Even nowadays this dreaded disease, which mainly strikes children and teenagers, can be fatal or cause permanent brain damage. Back in the 1920s, before antibiotics and other wonder drugs, meningitis had no treatment or cure. When Dom slipped into a coma shortly after being admitted, there was nothing his doctors could do for his condition but advise my parents to pray.

Momma and Papa certainly didn't need any encouragement to do that. Every morning they left for the hospital in hopeful anticipation, but their faces were always strained when they returned home in the late afternoon.

I was only seven, but I knew Dom was very sick. "We sit beside him talking," I heard Momma telling one of my sisters. "For hours. But he can't open his eyes. Or make a sound. Or even move a finger." Papa put his arms around her as she leaned against his chest, softly weeping.

Like our parents, we children prayed hard for Dom to recover. My prayers were sincere, but I have to admit that with each passing day my faith began to weaken. *God, why aren't You making Dom well? This has been going on for so long.*

Then, on the seventeenth day of his coma, Dom's face began to turn blue. His lungs were failing; his heartbeat was weaker. Dom was dying.

Momma and Papa sat with him for hours, holding his hands and praying. Then they returned home, exhausted from the emotional and physical stress.

I had just gotten back from school when I saw Momma and Papa come in. They were so sad and tired they barely spoke. Momma went right to the bedroom and lay down; when I looked in a minute later she was fast asleep. While resting on the couch in the living room Papa had fallen sound asleep too. As I played idly with a doll on the kitchen floor, I looked at the dust motes drifting in the late afternoon sunlight. Why wasn't God making Dom better? Weren't all those prayers from all those people helping? I uttered another one of my own, from deep within my being: "God, please, make my brother well."

I sat in silence for a few minutes, a shiver building along the back of my neck. From far away I heard a dog bark, a window open, a neighbor call out. Then suddenly the stillness was broken. Papa woke with a start. He gave a cry like I had never heard before—"Assunta! Assunta!"—and leaped to his feet. He raced toward the bedroom. At the same time Momma had awoken abruptly and leaped out of bed. As I sat on the floor in wonderment, my parents rushed at each other from opposite ends of the house and met in the hallway right in front of me.

"Paulo!" Momma cried. "I just had a dream! I had been praying before I fell asleep and I know the message was from God. A voice told me, 'Go to the hospital! Now!'"

I will never forget the shock in my father's voice. "Assunta, just moments ago I had the same dream. I also heard those words: 'Go to the hospital! Now!'" He threw his arms around my mother. "Hurry!" he said.

My parents rushed to the hospital and went straight to my big brother's room. Dom was sitting upright. He had just come out of the coma. With a weak but clear voice, he said with a smile, "I want some ice cream."

He had recovered. The doctors were astounded. They discharged Dom soon afterward. He went on to live a full, healthy life of eighty years.

Dom later told me that while lying in the coma, he had experienced a vision that forever took away his fear of death. But he didn't tell anyone exactly what it was he saw. He only said, "I will never be afraid to die. God is good, and I will trust in Him forever."

Many events have occurred in my life since, some involving illness and great disappointment and loss. But my parents' miraculous dreams on that June afternoon gave me the knowledge that God directs our lives in ways we cannot begin to fathom.

And, like Dominick, I will trust Him forever.

IN THE ARMS OF LOVE

DEBBIE RHODES

The sweet smell of peanut butter cookies filled my kitchen that cold day in January. The warmth of the oven was a contrast to the rainy winter storm raging outside my window. The sounds of children playing floated down the hall from their rooms. With three of them, our lives were filled with love and a constant flutter of activity. I had had difficulty getting pregnant, and so as each child came to our family, we felt very lucky. After having two healthy sons, we were given our precious daughter. Born the day after Christmas, she was a very welcome gift that year.

All morning the boys, Brian and Eric, had been chanting, "We want more peanut butter cookies! We want peanut butter cookies!" I had promised them that just as soon as they cleaned their rooms, we would share our favorite treat together. But after a few minutes, I could tell by the sounds down the hall that there was more playing than cleaning going on. I walked down to the boys' room to encourage them to "get with it" and realized that our daughter, Amy, was not with them. Immediately my mind went to our backyard. As I opened the back door, I caught sight of something in the Jacuzzi. Floating facedown in the water was my precious two-year-old daughter. I pulled her out of the cold water by the back of her little overalls and looked down into her face: it was white, cold and lifeless.

I don't have the words to describe the pain I felt as I held this little darling in my arms. Running through the house I screamed, "Call 911. Hurry, Brian, your sister has drowned! Call 911!" I ran out the front door, carrying Amy's limp, wet body as I yelled for anyone to help. Through the bushes and into the neighbor's yard I ran, shouting, "Help me, please, somebody help me!" My neighbors, Dodie and Al, were seldom home during the day, but thank goodness they were there this day. Dodie took Amy from me and dropped her to the grass, instinctively administering mouth-to-mouth resuscitation as I helplessly watched and prayed for my daughter's life.

Soon friends and neighbors gathered around us. Dodie and Opal, another good friend, took turns doing CPR. Amy was still not breathing. My baby wasn't breathing! Within about twenty minutes the sheriff's department arrived and began CPR, but still no sign of life. I held Amy's hand as we rushed to the hospital while the sheriff tirelessly continued the CPR. The San Bernardino County Hospital was only a short distance away, and the minute we arrived, a team of doctors took Amy into the emergency room. Never had I prayed so hard, so sincerely.

Amy's heart had not been beating for over half an hour. I knew what that meant, and all those thoughts began to overwhelm me as I waited alone for my husband, Mark, to get to the hospital. After forty-five agonizing minutes, the doctor told me that Amy's heart was beating again, but that a machine was doing the breathing for her.

Mark finally arrived at the hospital, not knowing the severity of the situation. A he looked at his daughter in her desperate condition—tubes in her mouth, nose, arms, and a breathing machine giving her life—he was devastated. He immediately called a friend from our church and, along with Amy's uncle Doug, gave her a special blessing of healing, in accordance with the custom of our religion. As the beautiful words came forth, a sense of peace settled over us. We suddenly felt comfort in the knowledge that Amy was in God's hands—she was encircled in the arms of His love, and for the first time that day, we felt hope.

The chief neurologist at the hospital, Dr. Ashwal, came over to us and said, "I don't even know you, but I do know of your strong faith and family support. If I could just say one thing, it would be to hold on to that faith to help you get through this experience. If Amy makes it through the first seventy-two hours, there is a ninety-eight percent chance she will live, but there will be brain damage to deal with. She'll be in the pediatric intensive care unit for three to four months, with a minimum cost of eighty thousand dollars, and then she'll be in basic care for an undetermined length of time." I was in shock. No matter which way we looked at it, the prognosis was grim.

Every measure was taken to save Amy's life. The staff worked on her constantly while she lay in a deep coma. The drugs, the tube placed through her tiny neck, a steel bolt inserted into her shaved head—all the finest medical technology was used in an effort to bring our child back. I felt immeasurable gratitude for this incredible team of doctors, but I still cried when they brought me Amy's beautiful blond curls in a small, brown paper bag.

During that first seventy-two hours, a special nurse had been assigned to us. At one point during the night, as she and I stood alone together in the intensive care unit, I pleaded with this woman to be completely honest with me. I needed to know the truth about Amy's prognosis; I needed to be prepared. She looked at me with hesitation but with great compassion as she spoke the words I was dreading: "I have worked with over a hundred drowning patients. Of all of them, no one with a pH level as low as 6.6 like Amy's has ever lived. Not one. A few with a pH of 6.8 have lived, but as vegetables. You may want to consider whether or not you want her life to continue in that manner."

So there it was. A truth shared in the darkness of the night between two women . . . two women who, in their own separate lives, had been profoundly touched and forever altered by the experience of loving and caring for a child . . . two mothers.

Amy looked so sweet and peaceful as she lay in the coma. It was comforting just to be in her presence. But I soon found out the impossibility of being content with just that as I began to envision a lifetime of such an inert existence. I ached to hear the sound of her small voice when I would ask her, "Are you Mama's baby?" to which she would tease, "No! Da-da's baby!" We would play this game over and over, and every time she would squeal with delight.

Our little fighter made it through those critical seventy-two hours. Dr. Ashwal met us early the next morning. He wanted to try to take her out of the coma, but there were many risks. We could lose her altogether, but the alternative of leaving her in a coma seemed like a cruel sentence. The doctor explained that if he attempted this procedure, we probably wouldn't see any movement or eye function for several days. It would be a long, slow process, and we needed to be patient.

Mark and I stood on either side of Amy's bed as the tubes were removed. Around noon she was taken off the drugs that had kept her in the coma and had kept her alive. Again, the doctor warned us that it would be many days, if at all, before we might notice any change in Amy. Yet there we stood—waiting, hoping.

In not more than one hour, Amy's eyes suddenly opened. She looked up at me and said the most beautiful words I had ever heard: "Mama, Mama, Mama." In disbelief, Mark called her name and she turned to him and said, "Da-da," and then closed her eyes once again.

Amy's nurse was in the room with us. Breathlessly, she exclaimed, "I can't believe it! This is incredible!" At that moment, we all knew that God had given us a miracle.

Amy left the pediatric intensive care unit the next day, not even one full week after her accident. All of us around her who had been prepared to endure three or four months of painful, anxious waiting agreed as the doctor proclaimed, "What a miracle. We attribute this to a power greater than us all."

Fifteen years later, Amy is still a miracle and a blessing to our family. As I look at her amazing life now, I sometimes think about where Amy might have gone during those first few lifeless moments after the drowning. Could she have spoken to God? And if so, might they have discussed whether it was time for her to go home to Him or whether there was still work to do and people's lives to touch here on earth? I don't know the answers to those questions, but I somehow know that during those few precious moments, He must have tenderly picked her up and, cradling her in the arms of His love, brought her back to us.

A PERFECT CHILD

KATHLEEN LUKENS

Quite unexpectedly one day, a close friend surprised me by announcing her plans to go to Lourdes to bathe her young handicapped son in the curative waters. Marie was a Catholic and, to many Catholics, the French city of Lourdes is a place for miraculous cures. She saved up for the trip for a solid year.

Marie and I had helped each other through our late thirties. Her Billy and my David were born brain-damaged. They were both the fourth of five children, and a unique source of joy and grief. Marie and I had been through many trials together.

It would be a difficult trip for her alone, with an unpredictable seven-year-old; in addition, she'd never been out of the country and didn't speak a word of French. But even if there was only a slim chance that the waters of Lourdes would miraculously help Billy and transform him into a normal child, she must have felt she owed it to him to try.

We didn't discuss it much before she left. When I asked if I could help with her other children, she said everything was taken care of. Then Marie and Billy were gone.

Almost before I had time to miss her, Marie returned. She came back with a spring in her step and a new vitality in running her teeming household. She was more patient. There was a peace about her.

Billy, on the other hand, seemed exactly the same.

I was puzzled. As the weeks went by, I kept expecting Marie to tell me what had happened at Lourdes. But I didn't dare ask. The trip had obviously been a private experience. She didn't have to come out and tell me of her inner struggle. I knew.

I loved my David, but I wanted him to be like other kids. How often had I thought, *Wouldn't it be wonderful if David were a normal child? A completely different child?* Other parents might wish their sons were better students or more athletic, their daughters less moody or more ambitious. Those weren't monumental changes, like what I wanted for David. What I wanted for my son would take a miracle.

Then one day while I was visiting Marie, she went up to her room and came back carrying a small plastic bottle. "Here, Kathy," she said. "I brought you some Lourdes water."

I held the container tightly in my palm and searched Marie's eyes. Maybe she was ready to talk. "Do you think it worked for Billy?" I asked.

Marie looked away.

Suddenly I felt terrible; of course it hadn't worked for Billy. How could I be so cruel?

"You don't understand," Marie said slowly, "I didn't dip him in the waters."

"You *didn't*?"

"I couldn't," she said. "When it came time to do it, I just couldn't."

Mental pictures of Marie dropping coins and one-dollar bills into a mayonnaise jar, week after week, to save up for the trip; the ten-hour plane ride, plus hours on the train; the stress on her family; her expectations—all passed through my mind. How could she have refused such an opportunity if she truly believed that a miracle might take place?

The word came out in a whisper. "Why?"

"Because I love him the way he is."

All at once, I understood. I recognized the source of the peace Marie had discovered.

"Even if he'll never be the way I dreamed he'd be," Marie said, "I still love my son."

A healing *had* taken place at Lourdes. And now it touched me. My child was from God. If someday, by some miracle, David were different, or "normal," I would praise God for his healing. And I'd love David—but no more than I love him at this very moment.

TOUCHED BY HEAVEN'S HAND

KELSEY TYLER

There has always been something special about Bill and Becky Harter's fifth child, Scotty. The ten-year-old is quiet when his siblings are rambunctious; serious when they are silly. And above all, he is sensitive to spiritual matters and the feelings of others.

In some ways Scotty's personality makes Becky understand better the miracle of his life, and how but for God's healing touch he might not have lived to see his third birthday.

Becky knew nothing of the problems her son faced until shortly after his birth. The pregnancy had been normal, and on a beautiful fall day in Tempe, Arizona, in 1985, William Prescott Harter entered the world without complications. Almost immediately everyone called him Scotty.

Becky, a longtime nurse, had struggled with past pregnancies, and by the time Scotty was born she had suffered six miscarriages in addition to the births of her four older children. She knew for certain that Scotty would be her last, and in the morning after he was born, her arms ached to hold her newborn son.

Minutes slipped away and Becky began to wonder why Scotty hadn't been brought to her. When she was about to contact someone and ask about her baby, a nurse practitioner entered her room. The woman was a friend of Becky's, and as she approached the hospital bed, Becky saw that her face was stricken.

"Becky, I'm so sorry," she said. Tears filled her eyes.

Becky felt her heart stand still.

The nurse practitioner paused for a moment. "I examined Scotty's charts and records. There's something wrong with his heart."

"That's impossible. They checked him right after he was born and everything was fine."

Becky searched for a way to make sense of the information.

Sandy shook her head. "They did some more tests. I'm sure about this, Becky. There's something very seriously wrong with his heart."

Becky studied her friend, knowing that she would not bring this type of bad news unless she was certain. Sandy had delivered a stillborn baby not long ago and Becky had helped her survive the grief. She was sure that Sandy would not suggest such a diagnosis unless it was true.

"Has the doctor seen the results?" Becky asked, her voice strained.

Sandy nodded. "He'll be here in a little while to talk with you. I thought you might want to hear it from me first."

Becky nodded and Sandy could see that she was partially in shock. The women hugged each other and then Sandy disappeared back into the hallway. Immediately she telephoned Bill and asked him to come to the hospital as soon as possible.

Shortly after Bill arrived, the pediatrician entered the room.

"I'm sorry to have to tell you this, but Scotty appears to have a large hole between the left and right chambers of his heart. Blood is passing abnormally from one chamber to the other," he said.

Becky tightened her grip on Bill's hand. "What exactly does this mean, doctor?" Bill asked, his brow furrowed.

"It is very, very serious. Ideally, if the baby survives beyond his second birthday, we would do open heart surgery then to repair the hole. However, if he begins to show signs of respiratory failure or heart failure, we would have no choice but to operate right away. In that case, babies rarely survive."

Questions raced through Becky's mind: *What did we do wrong, God? Why is this happening to us?*

Meanwhile the doctor explained that the next series of tests would not be performed until Monday.

"Because you are a trained nurse, Becky, you can take Scotty home with you this weekend. But watch for signs of cyanosis, blue skin, difficulty breathing, drawing in the chest area."

"You mean he might not live through the weekend?" Bill sounded incredulous. Two years was precious little time, but now it seemed the doctor doubted whether Scotty would live through the week.

"Yes, I'm afraid so. Many times children born with this type of heart defect don't live more than a few days." He turned toward Becky. "Do you think you can handle having him at home for a few days?"

Becky nodded absently, silent tears slipping down her cheeks. Bill put his arm around her shoulder and drew her near. The doctor bid the couple good-bye and left.

"What do we do now?" Becky looked up into Bill's eyes, searching for answers. Bill sighed. "We take him home and do the only thing we know how to do," he said. "We pray for a miracle."

As they drove home with Scotty, Bill and Becky made a decision to keep the dreaded news from the other children. They also decided not to tell well-meaning friends and distant family members. Only Becky's parents, who were strong Christians, and six of their closest friends would know the truth about Scotty's heart.

"I don't want the children to be sad at a time when they should be joyously welcoming their new brother," Becky explained as she talked to her mother that evening. "And we don't need a lot of people grieving with us. Right now we want to pray for a miracle and expect that one will happen."

That weekend was a series of intense hours of prayer alternated with quiet moments alone with Scotty. On his first night home, Becky rocked her newborn son long into the early morning hours, whispering hopeful words of encouragement and telling him how much God loved him.

"Jesus will heal you, little Scotty," she said. And then in a silent voice she added, *Please, God, know that we are standing on Your promises. We believe with all our hearts that You will heal our son. Please, God.*

Then she stared at Scotty, sobbing softly and memorizing his face, wondering if that would be the last night she would ever spend rocking him to sleep.

Bill joined her before going to bed, and put a soothing hand on Becky's shoulder.

"He's going to be okay, honey," he whispered. "I really believe God is going to heal him."

Becky shook her head and cried harder. Her faith was weaker than it had ever been in her life, and she couldn't find the strength to believe as strongly as Bill did that things would work out all right for Scotty.

"I'm afraid I'm going to lose him, Bill. I understand how serious that type of heart defect is and maybe God wants him in Heaven for some reason."

Bill nodded. "I know, honey. But deep inside I have a feeling he's going to be okay. It's something I can't explain."

Becky sniffed loudly. "Good. At least one of us is believing. And, Bill, pray that I might believe it, too."

The next morning, Becky woke feeling as if a burden had been lifted from her shoulders. She checked on Scotty and found him sleeping peacefully, and suddenly her heart soared.

"As if God was trying to reassure me that you were right," she told her husband later that morning. "Scotty is going to be fine, even though it doesn't make sense right now."

On Monday morning, Becky bundled Scotty into a receiving blanket and she and Bill carried him into the office of a pediatric heart specialist. The man had been to the hospital to see Scotty the day after his birth and had confirmed the diagnosis at that time. Now he wanted to run specific tests to determine the exact severity of the hole between the chambers of Scotty's heart.

Throughout the morning technicians performed a series of tests on Scotty while the Harters waited anxiously to talk with the specialist. Finally, they were called into an examining room where the doctor was going over the test results. His face was a mask of gravity as he put them down and approached the infant.

"How's he been acting this weekend?"

Becky smiled nervously. "Fine, actually. Nursing and sleeping well, his color has been normal."

The doctor nodded and donned a highly sensitive stethoscope. He listened closely to Scotty's heart, and then turned him onto his stomach and listened again, this time through his back. Once more he repeated this procedure until finally he stood up straight and sighed.

"All I can say is, I'm sorry," he said, shaking his head.

For an instant Becky felt the color drain from her face and she gripped Bill's hand. He's dying, she thought. The doctor's going to tell us Scotty's dying.

Instead, the doctor continued. "I would never, ever have made this diagnosis if I wasn't one hundred percent certain." He stopped for a moment, searching for words. "There is no explanation for this except that a miracle must have happened."

Becky caught her breath and waited for the doctor to continue.

"What are you saying, doctor?" Bill asked, daring to believe the impossible.

The doctor glanced once more at the most recent test results. "This baby is perfectly normal. There's nothing wrong with Scotty."

Becky began to cry and clutched Scotty tightly to her chest. "Thank You, God, thank You," she muttered softly into the child's ear.

Bill struggled to find his voice, his eyes brimming with unshed tears. "Where do we go from here? Should we watch for any symptoms or have more tests done in a few months?"

The doctor lifted his eyebrows, at a loss for an explanation. "There simply is no hole between the chambers of his heart. It's disappeared completely." He smiled and ran a finger gently over Scotty's cheek. "All you need to do now is take him home and love him."

For months Scotty's case was studied by teams of specialists. Each time they tried to understand how a hole that had clearly shown up on tests taken at birth had somehow disappeared two days later. Finally, the case was recorded as without medical explanation.

Every now and then, when Becky watches Scott playing basketball with his friends or talking heart to heart with his father, she remembers how he almost missed out on life altogether. It's at times like those that she knows she has the only answer that makes sense.

"God heard our prayers and in His perfect will He answered us with a miracle. Our very own miracle baby."

Chapter 2   The Gift of Health Restored

As Jesus approached Jericho, a blind man was sitting by the roadside begging. When he heard the crowd going by, he asked what was happening. They told him, "Jesus of Nazareth is passing by."

He called out, "Jesus, Son of David, have mercy on me!"

Those who led the way rebuked him and told him to be quiet, but he shouted all the more, "Son of David, have mercy on me!"

Jesus stopped and ordered the man to be brought to him. When he came near, Jesus asked him, "What do you want me to do for you?"

"Lord, I want to see," he replied.

Jesus said to him, "Receive your sight; your faith has healed you." Immediately he received his sight and followed Jesus, praising God. When all the people saw it, they also praised God (Luke 18:35-43, NIV).

When we find ourselves in need of healing, we are usually at the end of our rope and just hanging on. We are desperate, and we will pester anyone who can possibly offer relief: doctors, nurses, therapists, pastors, even Aunt Sylvia's neighbor's cousin, who knows someone at Johns Hopkins. While suffering in silence makes a fine martyr, most of us are not prepared to march silently into martyrdom. We discuss and argue and nag, seeking the answer we want, which is healing. When the blind man sitting on the road to Jericho heard the commotion of crowds and found out that it was Jesus who was walking, he started shouting for Him to stop. People told him to be quiet, but he just continued shouting, raising the decibel level to get the Healer's attention. When Jesus stopped and asked him what he wanted, our hero was ready with his answer: "Lord, I want to see." Clear, concise and to the point. This man knew what he wanted.

We too are often told to be quiet, to face reality: healing is not available to us, no matter how loudly we shout or who we ask, or so the experts say. But God does respond to our cries, and when He asks us what we want, we need to be very clear: we want healing. For it is our faith that heals us, as the people in the following stories can testify.

Father, You do not protect us against catastrophes but in them You come to our aid. It is in the very midst of the tempest and misfortune that a wonderful zone of peace, serenity and joy bursts in us if we dwell in Your grace. You do not help us before we have helped ourselves, but when we are at the end of our resources You manifest Yourself, and we begin to know that You have been there all the time.

—Louis Evely

EXPECT A MIRACLE

DAWN STOBBE, AS TOLD TO MEG LUNDSTROM

Wherever I go, I carry a small gray stone. It's in my purse all day, tucked under my pillow each night. And on it are painted three simple words: Expect a Miracle. I did expect one, and against all odds, that's exactly what I was given.

A year ago, when I first had bloating and pains in my pelvis and lower abdomen, I passed it off as side effects from the estrogen I was taking for menopause. But driving home one day, the pain got so wrenching I nearly crashed my car.

This can't be normal! I thought in fear. I'm a nurse, so I raced to my medical books as soon as I got home. Almost as if I were directed, I picked one from the shelf and opened straight to the page on ovarian cancer. A chill raced down my spine as I read the symptoms—bloating, pain, frequent urination . . . I had every one.

"We'll have to run some tests," my doctor said after examining me. "But it could be ovarian cancer."

Driving home, I felt so scared I could barely breathe. And when I walked in the door, my husband, Rich, took one look at me—and hugged me close. "We just need to pray," he told me.

But my test results were terrifying: I had a large tumor, and a blood test that indicated the possible presence of ovarian cancer read 462—normal is thirty. *I'm going to die!* I wept.

That night, I forced myself to stay calm as I told our two teenage daughters that I had cancer. But when I saw the fear in their eyes, my heart nearly broke in two. So I wouldn't burden them with my fear, I said I had to run to the store and slipped out to my car, tears coursing down my cheeks.

In my mind, I pictured all the faces I loved: Rich, the girls, our five other children through previous marriages, parents, friends. . . .

Oh, God, please don't take my life, I pleaded. *I still have so much to live for.*

"Don't do this alone," my priest told me when I cried to him. "Let others help you." And the next day, all those faces I pictured the night before were in my home, surrounding me with their love.

Their love carried me through my surgery to remove the tumor, along with my fallopian tubes and ovaries. But I was far from out of danger. "You still have only a fifteen percent chance of making it," one doctor told me. "Your only hope is chemotherapy."

Half-crazed with fear, I began making frantic bargains: *If You heal me, God, I'll be a better wife, a better mom, a better person. Just give me a second chance.*

I had six chemo treatments, once every three weeks. Sometimes I thought I wouldn't make it through them, they made me so weak and sick. But when I most needed a boost, a friend would show up with dinner or drop by to take the girls out.

Folks even organized fund-raisers to help us pay my medical bills!

Buoyed by so much love, I knew I owed it to others—and to myself—to stay optimistic. So I read books on healing and listened to tapes that helped me visualize getting well. *I'm not giving in,* I'd think.

Rich was my strength whenever I felt afraid, praying with me and holding me. My daughters stayed positive, too. Lindsay, fourteen, and Sarah, sixteen, refused to believe I would die. "You're going to be all right, Mom," they'd say.

But after my last treatment, I faced a terrifying moment of truth. Doctors were going to take one hundred biopsies, one in every place they feared the cancer might have spread.

"To be honest, we don't expect to find you're cancer-free," they warned. And if the chemo hadn't destroyed the cancer cells, my chances for survival were slim.

I could feel terror creeping into every fiber of my being. *I can't give up hope now,* I thought fiercely. So before leaving for the hospital, I opened the drawer where I kept a good-luck symbol a friend had given me, a small, hand-painted rock. *Expect a Miracle,* I read, then slipped the stone in my purse.

The stone was still in my purse the next day, when I opened my eyes after surgery to find a pretty woman with dark hair and white dress leaning over my hospital bed. *She must be a nurse*, I thought. But she had no pills in her hand, no blood pressure monitor to hook up. Instead, she looked at me kindly and asked, "Are you the one who's looking for a miracle?"

Confused, I stammered, "Yes." *But how did she know?* I wondered. Then, before the question left my lips, she'd vanished.

The next morning, the woman in white was beside me once again. In her hand was a plaque that read: *Miracles Happen Every Day.* "Is this what you're looking for?" she asked gently.

Tears sprang to my eyes, but before I could say a word, once again she was gone. As I gazed at the plaque she'd given me, I felt a funny tingly sensation throughout my body.

"Dawn," Rich said as I groggily opened my eyes, "the results of the biopsies are in. They were negative—each and every one!"

I'll never know whether the woman was a nurse—or an angel. But it doesn't matter. She came to let me know that hopes are never foolish, prayers never wasted.

Today, I'm forty-nine and cancer-free. And each time I hug my daughters, share a quiet moment with Rich or just watch autumn leaves scuttle across the sidewalk, I remember again that every new day is a blessing, a new chance to expect a miracle.

COVERED WITH THE WORD

LINDA SHUBLAK

awoke early on November 30 last year wrapped in romantic thought. David and I had been married less than two months, and it was thrilling to open my eyes and find my handsome thirty-five-year-old husband doing his warm-up exercises beside the bed before his daily run. He leaned down, kissed me and slipped one of his two dog-tag chains around my neck. "Wear these till I come home," he whispered before he left.

David was a major in military intelligence at Fort Huachuca, and as I fingered his tags around my neck, I thanked God for bringing us together. Our marriage was the second for both of us, one we had long prayed about. Each of us had asked God for a lifetime Christian mate, and at last our dream had come true.

I glanced at the clock, jumped up and showered. I had joined a Red Cross class, and was training to become a volunteer at the post-dental clinic. Before leaving for class, I wrote David a love note. While I was taping it on the bathroom mirror, where he would see it when he came home to shower, I heard the wail of sirens. I paused to pray for whoever was injured, as I had done since I was a little girl. Then I went off to class, not realizing I had just prayed for my own husband.

I was in class when David's commanding officer appeared at the doorway and motioned for me to come into the hall. One look at his face told me something was wrong. He gave me the news as calmly as he could: "David was hit by a car while he was jogging."

As the colonel walked with me to the hospital adjacent to the dental clinic, I learned that David had been struck by a car traveling about fifty-five miles an hour. The driver had been temporarily blinded by the rising sun, and David had been thrown onto the hood, landing against the windshield. When the horrified driver hit his brakes, David was catapulted some sixty-four feet and landed headfirst on the pavement.

When we got to the hospital, medics were moving him onto a flight for the University Medical Center (UMC) in Tucson, seventy-five miles away. I was in a state of shock as the colonel's wife drove me there.

At UMC's emergency room I was told David would be taken to surgery to repair his broken legs and arm. But then a neurosurgeon appeared and canceled those plans. David's head scans showed he had suffered multiple skull fractures, and little brain activity was going on. They would have to put in a shunt immediately to relieve pressure on his brain, and use a monitor to gauge his intracranial pressure moment by moment.

The neurosurgeon looked directly into my face. "Your husband is dying," he said. "He has two to forty-eight hours, at most."

I wanted to scream at him or ask if he could be wrong. But I had always been too polite to question people in authority. That's what Holleigh, my twenty-one-year-old daughter from my previous marriage, said anyway. She always tried to get me to stand up for myself. But the doctor was towering over me now. "You should call your family and get them here fast," the neurosurgeon was saying. "And I see your husband marked 'donor' on his driver's license, so you'll need to think about donating his organs."

Suddenly the room seemed to be closing in. I had to get outside. "Thank you," I said. "Excuse me. I have to go pray now." I stumbled to an outside patio and sank down onto a bench. *How can this be happening? How can David be dying?*

My mind escaped to the previous June, to the tranquil front porch of my lakefront house in Sackets Harbor, New York, where David and I had met. I was living a quiet life with Holleigh, and David was on a four-month assignment in the area. I sat reading my Bible on the front porch as David ran by each morning. One day he stopped and started a conversation about the Bible, which led to dating and a proposal soon afterward. We both recognized each other as God's answer to our prayers for a lifetime mate.

By the time David's father, mother and brother Mark arrived at the hospital, I was fasting and praying—sometimes silently, sometimes murmuring softly into

David's ear while I held his hand—hour by hour. A kind neurosurgeon, Dr. William D. Smith, was now on David's case, but the prognosis was still bleak. When doctors shone a light in David's eyes, there was no response. Soon David sank into coma.

The pressure on David's brain shot up to five times above normal the next day. Dr. Smith explained that since the brain was swelling and pushing against the skull, circulation was being cut off; my husband's brain was being damaged to such an extent that, if he lived, he would be a vegetable.

Forty-eight hours passed. Dr. Smith told us the monitor showed pressure on the brain that was incompatible with life. "Clinically, your husband is brain dead," he explained gently.

On the fifth day after the accident, when David's condition did not change, well-meaning friends drew up a list of how many of his organs could be used to help those in dire condition. Arrangements were made for David to be buried at Arlington National Cemetery. I understood the others' motivation. I had put my husband in God's hands and would accept whatever happened. But I couldn't shake the feeling that neither God nor I was ready to give him up.

That evening, December 4, Dr. Smith called the family together. Gently but firmly he explained that we could continue to keep David on life-support indefinitely or we could make the decision to harvest his organs. Holleigh joined us as the family talked it over into the night, our hearts breaking.

When I went to my room, I felt lower than ever. Tears streaming down my face, I took my Bible to bed. *God, if David is truly dead and it's Your will that he be with You, I understand. But if there's something more I should do, please let me know.*

I opened my Bible to the Book of John. And there was the story of Lazarus. I had read it many times before, but suddenly the words took on new meaning. Martha's brother, Lazarus, had been dead for four days when Jesus went to the tomb with Martha. As I read, my tears stopped abruptly. "I am the resurrection and the life," Jesus said, "he who believes in me, though he die, yet shall he live . . . Do you believe?" (John 11:25-26, RSV).

I sat up in bed. "Yes, I believe!" I said aloud. "I believe that if it's Your will, You can save David now just as You saved Lazarus then!"

The next morning I dressed in the brightest-colored clothes I had, as a symbol of life. Carrying my Bible as if it were a sword, I went into David's room to battle for his life. As usual, he was lying spread-eagled on that strangely shaped bed, which moved constantly to stimulate his circulation.

Maneuvering carefully around all the tubes and medical apparatus, I started reading the eleventh chapter of John, standing over David's head, then on one side of him, then on the other side of him, and at his feet, even kneeling and leaning under his bed. I was not trying to perform some magical ritual. Rather, I was trying to cover David's body with the Word of God. Doctors and nurses in the room gave me sidelong glances—a few openly disdainful, a few embarrassed and a few understanding. But I wasn't timid. I read aloud confidently.

When I finished reading, I opened my Bible and laid it on David's chest—the same Bible that had attracted David to me in Sackets Harbor. With my hands on his head, I prayed aloud for a miracle, heedless of the medical people looking on. While I sang "Amazing Grace," David's favorite hymn, his father stood by the window, his hands clasped in prayer, and his brother, Mark, prayed in the chapel. Medical teams came and went.

A neurosurgeon stopped me in the hall afterward. "Get a grip on reality," she told me. "Stop talking about miracles!"

For someone usually so awed by authority, I wasn't the slightest bit intimidated. "Our God is a mighty healer," I replied simply. All that day when anyone referred to David as brain-dead, I was surprised at the authority in my voice when I gave them the same response. Reports of others praying for David bolstered me even more.

When I went to the hotel room that night, I slept peacefully.

The next day as I walked into David's room, his father met me at the door.

"Don't get your hopes up," he said. "But when they examined David's eyes today they saw a flicker of response."

We sat watching and praying at David's bedside. As the hours passed, his arms moved, then later, his legs. On December 7, I wrote in my diary while sitting at David's side: "Buzzers and beeps resound in my husband's room—signs of life to all who hear that Jesus Christ is the healer!"

Gradually David responded more and more to what was going on around him.

He couldn't talk because he had a tube in his throat, so he wrote notes to his family clustered around his bed. With a shaky hand, he scrawled out to me: "I love you."

The neurosurgeons were all astounded by the reversal of David's condition. They said they had never seen anyone so badly injured return to normal. Dr. Smith said he had never seen a miracle, but he thought he was seeing one now. When the tube was removed from David's throat, he murmured that I was beautiful and asked me to marry him. "We *are* married," I said, laughing for the first time in days. On December 8, doctors repaired the breaks in David's legs and then his arm. Shortly after, David was moved to the Tucson Veterans Administration Medical Center.

Day by day, little by little, his memory returned—starting with his earliest behavior and progressing onward. David fast-forwarded in a matter of days from childhood (where he used crayons and played with little cars), through high school and into college (where he sang the Indiana University anthem) to adulthood, where he regained most of his intellectual capacity.

As Holleigh and I helped David get ready to go home on February 2, a new nurse inadvertently placed his legs in an awkward position in the wheelchair. I politely but firmly corrected her, and my daughter smiled. "I'm proud of you, Mom," Holleigh said later. "You stand up for yourself these days."

I fingered the dog tags around my neck, the ones I had never removed. Yes, I had stood up for what I believed in. And now my husband was coming home.

HEALED OVERNIGHT

QUIN SHERRER

When Nick Lovitt was twenty-five, he broke a bone in his left foot as he tripped over a grocery cart. It quickly developed into painful rheumatoid arthritis. If you saw the successful Colorado real estate broker today, you would have no clue how crippled he once was.

He shares his story:

Within forty-eight hours after I broke my left foot, gout set in. Over the next two years as it progressed, three different doctors diagnosed my condition as "gouty rheumatoid arthritis." The joints swelled in my left leg—foot, toes, ankle, knee and hip. Calcium spurs developed on the bottom of both feet and in my left ankle and knee.

I was taking three of the most powerful pain drugs available. In addition, I swallowed thirty to forty aspirins a day, but the medication did not suppress all my intense pain.

When I stood for the first time each morning, the torturing pain felt like nails being driven into the bottoms of my feet. The big toe on my left foot swelled to two inches in diameter and the left ankle to fourteen inches in circumference, twice its normal size. I couldn't walk without a cane.

My ability to function in real estate was greatly impaired. I would drive my customers to a house and let them walk through to see it themselves, to save myself the pain of standing. After two and one half years of this—even while taking in excess of eighty pills a day—I knew I could not endure the pain much longer.

On a November night in 1971, I was desperate. "Lord, I cannot go on with this pain and be a good father, husband and provider for my family. The pain is too much for me. I can't take it anymore. Lord Jesus, You must heal me or take me home. Please do something," I continued, sobbing like a baby.

I went to the medicine cabinet. As my wife watched in amazement, I flushed down the commode fourteen different bottles of pills plus two thousand aspirins. I was still sobbing and crying aloud. Then I went to bed not knowing what was going to happen.

The next morning I awoke on my back—a big switch after sleeping on my stomach for more than two years to avoid more intense pain. Something dramatic had happened in my body. I put my feet over the side of the bed and stood up immediately. No pain! No pain! No pain!

Cautiously, I walked out onto the tile floor. Then I ran outside, up and down the concrete sidewalk. Still no pain! I was crying, knowing I had been completely healed of gouty arthritis.

That very day I went back to the doctor and asked him to X-ray my feet. He compared them to previous X-rays, taken just two weeks before. He was astounded. Every calcium spur was gone. He had only one plausible explanation: Had I passed kidney stones—itself an excruciating ordeal?

"No," I told him pointedly, "I asked God to heal me."

"Medically, it is impossible for this to happen," he responded, still studying the two sets of X-rays. But God had performed my miracle instantly. In the twenty-five years since, I have not had a sign of recurrence.

The Miracle Worker is still at work—on duty night and day.

WHERE THERE IS HOPE

SARA RIVKA SASONKIN

At about 10:30 A.M. on the first of March [in 1994], a van carrying a group of young yeshiva scholars headed across the Brooklyn Bridge. Members of the Lubavitcher sect, they had just come back from a prayer vigil for their hospitalized leader, Rebbe Menachem Mendel Schneerson. Suddenly another car pulled abreast of them, and its driver fired a spray of bullets into their midst.

Amid shouts and screams the van screeched to a stop. The gunman sped off (he was captured the next day), leaving two boys shot in the head, slumped in the arms of their friends, and two others less seriously injured. One of those boys with a severe head wound was Nachum Sasonkin.

When my daughter Chani, who was living in Brooklyn, called to tell me Nachum had been hurt, I didn't believe it. I was born and raised in America, immigrating to Israel with my husband Avraham in 1962. I could not imagine the violence that had haunted my adopted country reaching out to claim my devout son, who had gone to America to study.

The hours after Chani's call passed in a kind of half-dream, half-nightmare. We had to find people to take care of the three children we still had living at home.

Other friends drove us to the Tel Aviv airport, and we caught a 1:00 A.M. flight to New York. How Avraham and I prayed on that plane!

At Kennedy Airport, policemen met us at the arrival gate and rushed us to St. Vincent's Hospital and Medical Center of New York. En route they explained that Nachum and his friends had been taken to this Catholic hospital because it was fully equipped to handle traumatic injuries such as head wounds.

None of this prepared us for our first sight of Nachum. He lay in the intensive care unit, his head swathed in bandages. His eyes were closed. There were tubes in his mouth and arm. He was breathing with the aid of a respirator. He looked asleep, but of course, no amount of begging or pleading would make him wake up.

Our fears worsened when we learned that the other boy with a head wound, Nachum's good friend Ari Halberstam, had died. Yet we clung to faith in God's mercy. In the hospital room a Hebrew saying flashed through my mind: *Even when the sharpest sword is on someone's neck, there is still hope.*

Outside the room we talked to Dr. Alan Hirschfeld, the neurosurgeon who had operated on Nachum. He explained how a bullet had struck our son in the back of the head, penetrating the cerebellum, the part of the brain that coordinates movement. Dr. Hirschfeld had removed the bullet and about fifteen percent of the cerebellum. But the injury caused the brain to swell, plunging Nachum into a deep

THE HIDDEN HAND OF GOD

coma. I shuddered to hear Dr. Hirschfeld say our son's chances of survival were not good. "On a scale of one to ten, I would give him a chance of point five," he said.

Another specialist who had examined Nachum gave us a far more negative report: "There's no chance for survival. Absolutely no chance."

I looked to my husband and other family members. None of us knew what to say or do. Only after the doctor departed did Avraham say in his quiet way, "God gives doctors permission to heal. He does not give them the gift of prophecy."

That was a turning point in our struggle to save Nachum. Our faith in God, our readiness to trust Him, which is the root of our life of prayer, returned with new intensity. We had been taught to make every moment of our daily lives part of our faith and worship. Now we asked God to bless our struggle to save Nachum in the same way.

Soon our hopes were anchored to tangibles. Nachum twitched when doctors or nurses gently pinched him. When I put my finger in his hand, he squeezed it exactly as he had done when he was a baby. Although his eyes remained closed, he was capable of responding to simple commands.

From the beginning Nachum was never alone. Day and night a family member or a friend from the yeshiva sat beside his bed, holding his hand, talking to him, reciting prayers, singing psalms.

At least as important were the prayers and concerns of the men and women of

St. Vincent's. The staff, led by Sister Karen Helfenstein, gave my husband and me an apartment in the hospital compound. They gave Nachum's friends a room near him, where they gathered daily to pray. They supplied us with kosher food. On Friday night they even turned off the smoke detectors near Nachum's room so we could light the candles that are an essential part of our Sabbath observance.

Over the next two weeks, Nachum slowly emerged from his coma. He opened one eye, then the other. Peering glassily, he recognized his brothers and sisters.

Nachum was still almost totally paralyzed, able to move only the fingers of his hand, when we launched a test to find out if his intellect was still intact. As part of his studies he had read countless volumes of our leader's writings. How would he respond to a basic question?

"Which volume of the Rebbe's writings has just been published?" my son-in-law asked him. "The thirty-first?"

Nachum's index finger wagged back and forth. No.

"Was it the thirty-second?"

Nachum's finger again indicated no.

"The thirty-third?"

Nachum moved his finger up and down. He had answered correctly. We were jubilant. The brilliant student was still in command of his mind.

Filled with joy, I found one of Nachum's friends, a young man who had been in the van when the bullets struck. He had held a wad of tissues to my son's bleeding head. "Nachum is going to live," I exclaimed. "He will marry and you are going to accompany us as we walk him to the marriage canopy!"

That was our faith speaking, strong and confident now, even though Nachum was still mostly in a coma, still on a respirator.

"*Baruch Hashem*," Nachum's friend said in Hebrew. *Thank God.* "*Baruch Hashem*," we all said in this Catholic hospital, with its statues and symbols that bear witness to God's mysterious mercy.

Slowly, painfully, over the next weeks, Nachum shook off his paralysis. He became fully able to move his hands and his legs. Not every day was a good one. There were setbacks. The muscles that controlled his ability to swallow often malfunctioned, and he developed infections in his lungs. We redoubled our prayers, and with the help of medication this threat was banished.

Soon Nachum was sitting up in bed, talking and laughing. He was able to breathe without the respirator. Finally the day came when he stood up and walked. Not well, I must admit. But it was still a miracle for a young man who had sustained an injury that kills ninety-five out of a hundred victims.

Today Nachum is at MossRehab Hospital in Philadelphia. A team of specialists works with him. Each day he makes progress. His speech is improving rapidly. He can now walk without a crutch or a helping hand. Everyone marvels at his determination. If he is told to perform an exercise ten times, he will do it twenty.

From the start Moss Rehab's goal was to help Nachum return to his Lubavitcher way of life. One of his first tasks was to relearn how to wrap the leather boxes and straps known as tefillin around his arm and head when he said his weekday morning prayers. His speech therapist has him study as they do in yeshiva. Nachum reads part of the Torah or another sacred text and then explains it to his father, who studies with him several hours every day.

Recently Nachum and I were discussing his calamity. We talked about how we do not understand the secrets of the universe, but we now know more intimately than ever God's readiness to respond to prayer and faith. I told Nachum that he would emerge from his ordeal a better man, stronger, more tolerant and more compassionate.

"*Baruch Hashem,*" he said.

Baruch Hashem, I repeated in my heart. *Thank God.* It will echo there a thousand times a day for the rest of my life.

CRASH!

JEREMY V. JONES

There are headlights in the lane in front of us! What do I do?"

Traveling eastbound on Interstate 76 near the Colorado-Nebraska border, seventeen-year-old Matt Weeden hit the brakes, but a patch of black ice offered no traction. Suddenly, his family's 1995 Dodge Intrepid was sliding sideways across the dark highway, completely out of control. It hit a sport utility vehicle in the lane beside them, then slammed into the back of an eighteen-wheeler parked on the shoulder. The windshield shattered into thousands of tiny pieces, and the airbags deployed.

The Weeden family was badly shaken, but seemed to be relatively okay since all three were wearing seat belts. Matt was unconscious and bleeding from the left side of his face but woke up as his parents tried to orient themselves in the cold night.

"Is anyone hurt?" shouted a paramedic. "Don't get out of the car!" Then he ran away.

"He's going to hit us!" Matt's father yelled.

A Dodge Ram pickup truck towing a camper slid across the ice and plowed into the already crumpled car. The second impact sent the Weedens' automobile into a 360-degree spin down the highway.

All three Weedens were knocked out. It took rescue crews more than two hours to cut off the crushed doors and peel back the roof to free the family. Larry and Beth, Matt's parents, faded in and out of consciousness as they waited, checking to make sure their son was still breathing.

With eleven vehicles eventually involved in the wreck, hospital space was scarce in this rural area. Matt and his parents were flown by Flight for Life helicopters about a hundred miles to Regional West Medical Center, a Class II trauma facility in Scottsbluff, Nebraska.

There Matt was diagnosed with a fractured skull, swelling and bleeding in the brain and a contusion of the brain stem. Both of his parents suffered broken shoulders and bruised or broken ribs. One of Beth's lungs was also collapsed. Even before the rescue crews had to cut it apart, their car was completely destroyed.

It was four days before Christmas 1999, but for Matt Weeden and his parents, their holiday trip to visit relatives in Wisconsin had changed in an instant. Only hours earlier, they had left their home in Colorado Springs. Now Matt was fighting for mental survival in a Nebraska hospital—and the whole family was just beginning a life-changing journey through trauma and healing that can only be described as miraculous.

The doctors in Scottsbluff provided excellent initial care in saving Matt's life and stabilizing him physically, but they were not used to dealing with the complexities of a closed head wound. Normal stimulation—TV, conversation, general noise—was too much for Matt's brain to handle. Only a couple of days after the accident, his symptoms began to escalate.

"With a closed head wound, the normal filters that we all have to keep us civilized in what we say and do are taken away," Larry said during an interview a couple of months later. "There's a tendency to get very irritable, very easily."

The normally good-natured, caring kid began using lots of profanity and making crude remarks to female nurses. He would wander the halls and shout "Get your hands off me!" when staff tried to guide him back to his room.

By the end of Christmas week, Matt had bitten a security guard and hit a technician with his lunch tray. One day, he took apart a disposable razor and belligerently refused to hand over the potential weapon. "That's when I knew that he was a danger to himself and others," Larry said. "His behavior scared me," Beth added. "I can honestly say I was afraid of him."

Larry and Beth began to fear that they might not get their good-natured, quick-witted son back. "There was no expression in his eyes. There was very little emotion except for anger," Beth said. "It was as if there was nobody in there."

Larry was alarmed by the seriousness of his son's injuries. "The doctors were talking about how it could take months, maybe years, to recover from a brain injury like this," he said later, "and that he might never be the same person again. That was frightening."

Though the future remained uncertain, Larry and Beth knew that God was protecting their family. "I don't know how any of you got out alive," a chaplain told them after seeing the wreckage of their car.

As soon as word got out about their accident, phone calls and e-mails began shooting across the country and around the world. The Weedens' former pastor called all the way from New Zealand to lend his support. Entire church congregations, friends and family, even strangers, began praying for the Weedens, especially Matt. "We really could feel those prayers and that God was working on our behalf," Larry said.

Of course, he and his wife were desperately seeking God themselves, asking Him to heal their only child. Larry remembers one particular prayer that he offered on Christmas day: "God," he said, "You know what it's like to have Your Son suffer. Would You please give me back my son?"

Matt's prognosis wasn't good, and the Weedens knew that only God could restore him completely. Beth remembers praying, "Lord, You are the Great Physician. You created Matt and know every part of his body. If healing is going to come, You've got to do it."

Although it was difficult for these parents to keep waiting, they took comfort in the care and support God provided through other Christians that they had never met before. Larry and Beth were discharged from the hospital within a week after the accident, but they remained in Scottsbluff because of Matt's critical injuries. During this time spent far from home, hospital chaplains and local pastors of all denominations rallied around them from the moment the Flight for Life helicopters landed. One family brought them presents and food on Christmas Day. Others offered their homes and cars for Larry and Beth to use once they were out of the hospital. Still more took care of needs like replacing broken eyeglasses and lost clothing. "It felt like an instant family," Beth recalled.

On December 29, eight days after the accident, Matt was transferred to Spalding Rehabilitation Hospital in Denver for more specialized treatment. He remembers being there but thinking it was all a dream. "I thought I'd been put in a mental institution, and I wanted to get out," Matt said later.

He tried everything he could to free himself. Some attempts were humorous—like trying to talk the nurses into giving him the "flashy thing" from *Men in Black* to heal him instantly. Other behaviors were much more serious—like trying to smash a chair through his window while yelling "I'm not crazy!"—or even worse, threatening to kill himself.

This continued for more than a week while Matt underwent both physical and mental therapy, but there were still no signs of progress. He continued to fixate on one thought at a time, and no one could talk logically with him. He was still unable fully to control his impulses. Though he could walk around, Matt couldn't even stand up when the doctors tested his ability to balance. While family and friends continued praying for recovery, Beth and Larry sang praise choruses with Matt each night, hoping to stir their music-loving son from within.

Finally, a breakthrough occurred. The day after his school forensics team dropped off a giant card at the hospital on January 8, Matt returned! "It was as if somebody had flipped a switch, and all of a sudden he was there again," Larry said. "The expression in his eyes and his sense of humor and everything were back," Beth added.

Despite his awakening, Matt needed further progress. He still had trouble focusing and concentrating. He also remained physically weak, needing to sleep after a little activity. "The future was still very uncertain at that point because when you have a brain injury like that, some of the cells are killed, and they don't regenerate," Larry said.

But Matt was determined to get out of that hospital, and he gave one hundred percent to reaching specific goals set by his therapists. He also spent every spare moment playing his guitar, an activity that helped his brain to practice concentrating.

Finally on January 12, twenty-two days after the accident, Matt was released from the hospital and ordered to undergo therapy for as long as necessary. But two and a half weeks later, his therapists and neuropsychologist all released Matt from their care. "The psychologist at Spalding said that he believes strongly in prayer and attributed Matt's progress to prayer," Beth related.

Matt returned to school just more than a week after being released from the hospital. Although he was still taking some medications to help him concentrate and deal with headaches, he quickly returned to normal activities like running three miles a day and competing—even winning—in forensics meets. He was forced to drop calculus, but was able to catch up on his French vocabulary words.

Larry and Beth have no doubt that it was God who performed Matt's healing. "His recovery has been so fast and so complete," Larry said. "We've heard of so many people who've had similar accidents and are still struggling with some of the effects for months, even years later. We don't know this side of heaven why God works one way in one person's life and another way in another's. The only reason for it is that God chose to heal Matt and answer those prayers."

Six months later, Matt's memories of the accident are still foggy, and he has no recollection of his first week at the hospital in Nebraska. Though doctors have proclaimed him fully recovered, Matt knows that his life has been changed after realizing just how short it can be for any of us. "I've been given a second chance in life, so I try to live the way I should, not being scared to talk about God to anyone," he says.

As for his parents, Larry and Beth know they've witnessed a miracle. After all, that miracle walks around their house every day.

THE INVISIBLE POWER

LLOYD S. DECKER

The diagnosis didn't sink in at first. *Visual acuity 20/400. Macular degeneration.*

Retinal vein occlusion. Legally blind.

For a year I'd been having trouble with my eyesight. New glasses and laser surgery hadn't made a difference. Still, I'd hoped some experimental treatment could correct the problem. But the specialists at the VA hospital told me nothing more could be done. Thirty years of high blood pressure had narrowed, then blocked, the central vein to the retina, damaging my vision permanently.

I let my wife, Erma, guide me out to our car. As she got behind the wheel, the seriousness of my situation started to hit me. Would I never write again? Never read a book?

That night I lay awake worrying. I had started to write a book after I retired from my career as an engineer. Would I have to give it up because I couldn't see well enough to read my computer screen?

The next morning I sat at the breakfast table, staring gloomily out at the back-yard. The world looked distorted, as if I were viewing it through dark-blue water. The straight iron railing on the deck was a snake shimmying in midair. The big oak tree had a trunk shaped like an *S* with its middle section erased.

Erma took my hand. "Remember what you tell people to do if they're in a jam?" she asked.

My answer was automatic: "When you're in trouble, pray."

"I always thought that was pretty good advice."

I nodded. But I didn't pray. What was the use? All my life, no matter how tough a situation I found myself in, I had been able to figure out something I could do to improve it. Sure, praying helped, but there was always some practical way to take action. This was different. If medical experts said nothing could be done, what could I hope for? Even with prayer.

As the days passed I fell deeper into despair. Our children, Bruce and Linda, called to cheer me up. When they put my grandchildren on the phone, I kept thinking about how I would never again see their faces brighten with smiles. Erma acted as if things hadn't really changed. But instead of enjoying retirement, she was working harder than ever taking care of me.

Then a relative gave me the phone number for Mike Cordero, a state case-worker for the blind. I gave him a call, not expecting much. We made an appointment. "I'm looking forward to meeting you," Mike said cheerfully. "We have a lot of work to do."

He seemed just as upbeat when he showed up the following Monday, sporting a jaunty pair of sunglasses. Mike broke the ice, chatting about his wife, their kids, how he'd taken them sailing over the weekend.

Why shouldn't he be happy? I thought resentfully. *His life is going just fine.*

"Now," Mike said, pulling a form out of his briefcase, "let me find out about you." He took off his sunglasses, brought the form an inch from his face and read the first question.

He's blind too! The dark glasses should have tipped me off, but I'd been too busy feeling sorry for myself to give them much thought. Even though Mike was disabled, he didn't act that way when it came to living his life.

A few days later he sent over a radio tuned to a station that broadcast newspaper articles, as well as a cassette player and a catalog of "talking books." I started listening to books-on-tape that I'd promised myself I would read someday. When I asked Mike where to get a magnifying glass powerful enough for me to read the print on my computer screen, he said, "I can do better than that."

He brought me software that enlarges letters up to sixteen times their original size. Working together, peering at the screen, we installed the new program. I typed in a few words. "I can read again!" I exulted. Soon I was back at work on my book. At no cost, the state furnished—through my friend Mike—all the technology I needed.

One morning I turned off the magnifying system by accident. I was about to reactivate it when I glanced at the screen. The words jumped at me—I could make them out, even thought the type was regular size!

Tests showed that the visual acuity in my right eye had improved dramatically, to a near-perfect 20/50. The doctor was puzzled. "Nothing in the structure of your eye has changed," he said. "There isn't any medical reason why you should be able to see all of a sudden. Yet you can, no doubt about it."

I told Erma, expecting her to be as stunned as I. "How did this happen?" I marveled. "I'm ashamed to admit it, but I haven't even been praying."

Erma smiled, looking happy but not surprised. "Maybe *you* haven't been praying," she said, "but other people have."

It turned out our son, Bruce, had asked the members of his church in New Hampshire to pray for me whenever they could—at services, meetings, classes. And they had been, for months.

As soon as I could, I was going to visit my son. I wanted to thank his friends for their prayers. First, though, I had to thank God for restoring what was most important—my belief in the power of prayer and, more than that, in *His* power. When I thought there was no hope, He brought Mike Cordero and the folks at my son's church into my life to show me there always is.

GOING FOR THE PRIZE

PAUL AZINGER

t takes a lot to get my mind off golf. Like most members of the Professional Golfers' Association, I eat, sleep and drink the game. That's the life of a pro. Or at least that's what I used to think.

Dr. Jobe called me unexpectedly on Friday evening after the second round of the 1993 PGA Championship at Inverness Club outside Toledo, Ohio. The PGA is a big tournament, one of the four Majors (along with the Masters and the U.S. and British Opens).

At the time, I had the dubious distinction of being known as the best player in the world never to win a major. Sure, I had come a long way from salad days struggling to make the qualifying cut at the PGA "tour school." Back at the 1987 British Open, I had the lead all week on the misty, windswept fairways of Muirfield in Scotland, only to suffer a devastating loss to Nick Faldo on the last hole. Though I won a lot of other tournaments, a major title still eluded me.

At age thirty-three, I was at the top of my game and feeling pretty invincible. I was in good shape going into the third round at Inverness, just a couple of shots off the pace behind Greg "the Shark" Norman, an Australian. My family was in Ohio with me, which made golfing even more of a pleasure. It was a heady feeling, competing for a $300,000 purse in front of a global TV audience. The pressure was definitely on. That's why it was strange that Dr. Jobe would call me at my hotel. My wife, Toni, handed me the receiver with a quizzical look and hushed the kids.

I had been having trouble again with nagging pain in my right shoulder. Dr. Jobe, one of the premier sports physicians in the world, had operated on my shoulder in 1991, and I had recently seen him in Los Angeles about the recurring soreness. Now he got right to the point: the X-rays he had taken concerned him. "Paul, I want you back in Los Angeles for a biopsy as soon as possible." *Biopsy?* I thought. *Is he crazy? I'm in contention here. I have the rest of the tour to finish and the Ryder Cup. I can't take time off now!*

Dr. Jobe finally relented and agreed that the biopsy could wait until later in the fall, when I would be in California for a tournament. Until then I would survive on anti-inflammatories, aspirin and prayer. *Tendinitis,* I told myself, and banished it from my mind.

I went out the next day, a boiling hot Saturday, and shot a solid sixty-eight to climb one stroke behind Norman. At the end of Sunday's final eighteen holes, I was in a tie with the Shark for the Wanamaker Trophy. Then, on the second hole of sudden-death play, Greg missed a tricky putt for par and I made mine to become the PGA champ. I had my title! Not one to take things mildly, I leapt into the air. Next

I gave thanks to the Lord, which is what I had always promised to do when I won a major. With Toni and our daughters, Sarah Jean, seven, and Josie, four, at my side, I went to raise the regal trophy high for all to see. Suddenly a sharp pain sliced through my right shoulder. It was all I could do to lift the silver cup.

I was determined not to let the pain lessen the thrill of victory or undermine my plans. I went to England and played with the United States team against the Europeans for the 1993 Ryder Cup, which we retained that year. But the pain never went away. By late November, when I finally saw Dr. Jobe in Los Angeles, I was barely able to operate the stick shift in my car. In fact, sometimes I drove and depressed the clutch while Toni shifted gears. As I sat on the table in Dr. Jobe's examining room that Monday morning at Centinela Hospital, showing him the spot on my shoulder that was now red-hot to the touch, he was irritated that he let me talk him out of doing a biopsy earlier. He took a pen and gently drew a line across the hot spot. "I'm going to make an incision right here," he said thoughtfully. "Don't shower that line off tomorrow morning."

As I dressed, for the first time I felt a stab of fear. *Come on, Zinger,* I reproached myself. *It's probably nothing.* That's what I told Toni that night back at the hotel while we talked quietly in our room and the kids went to dinner with Mildred, their sitter. What was the worst it could be? A stress fracture or some infection? I would be back on the course in no time. The next morning Dr. Jobe scraped out about a capful of tissue and bone for testing. We waited a few days for the results.

That week—a week of worry and prayer for Toni and me—I thought a lot about our life together and how intertwined with golf it was. We married in our home state of Florida in January 1982 as soon as I got my tour card, and Toni was a golf wife from the start. In those hard, early years Toni and I traveled the country in an old camper, chasing the tournaments. In the off-season back in Florida, she worked as a bookkeeper while I practiced, practiced, practiced. It might be my name up there on the leader board when I'm playing well, but really, Toni's should be there too. She's been as much a part of my success as I have.

When Toni and I went back to see Dr. Jobe, I dispensed with the usual pleasantries. "How am I?" I blurted out.

He looked at me right in the eye. "Paul, you have cancer."

One simple word. Cancer. Impossible. It was a good thing I was sitting. Toni gripped my hand and I rocked back and forth in my chair, shaking my head. I had been worried about my career, not about dying. Suddenly everything changed. "Paul. If the cancer is still localized, then it is treatable."

Something like a silent explosion overwhelmed me. "I need the restroom," I gasped, rushing out the door and down the hall. Bent over in that tiny bathroom, I put my head in my hands. I thought about Toni and the girls, about our life. I thought about golf. *Dear Lord, help me. I'm scared to death!* Then I cried until I heard Toni knocking on the door, asking gently, "Paul, are you okay?"

After I pulled myself together, Dr. Jobe brought me into see an oncologist, Dr. Lorne Feldman, who put me through a battery of tests to determine if the cancer had spread beyond my shoulder. Late in the day, Toni and I went back to our hotel to struggle through a weekend of waiting for the test results. As I played with the kids I thought about the PGA title, and what a cruel twist it would be if it turned out that I should have been in the hospital instead of competing with Greg Norman in the heat and humidity at Inverness.

We took Sarah Jean and Josie to a mall on Saturday to take our minds off our situation, but all the Christmas decorations going up just made me more anxious. Early Sunday morning a false fire alarm roused us from bed. Toni noticed a sign in the lobby announcing church services in one of the ballrooms. "Want to go?" she asked me.

Toni and I had become Christians back in the days when we were bouncing around the country in our old camper—happy, carefree, uncomplicated days, they seemed now. Sometimes it is when you have the least that you are most aware of how much the Lord provides. We always managed to put enough food in our mouths and gas in the camper. We took turns driving and reading aloud from the Bible.

Now Toni, Mildred, the kids and I slipped quietly into the back of the ballroom where services were being held by a local church, whose regular facilities were under construction. The big room was full and smelled of cut flowers. That false alarm had not been so false after all, for there was a fire in the air, a spiritual charge I felt throughout my body. I sensed I was face to face with God, and an excitement I hadn't felt in years came over me. I knew that Christ wanted not just my cancer, or my golf, or my fears about my family, but all of it—my whole life, if only I would give it to Him and recommit myself to faith. *I need You now more than ever, Lord,* I whispered silently.

That afternoon my parents flew in from Florida, and the next day we got the news from Dr. Feldman that as far as they could determine the cancer had not spread beyond the right scapula. I was immediately scheduled for six chemotherapy treatments, one every four weeks, administered right there in his office, starting that day. Between treatments I could return home to Florida.

That first chemo session was a doozy. I suffered intractable nausea and got so dehydrated that I had to be rushed back to the hospital for emergency treatment. But after a few days, Toni and I flew home. Coming home is always a relief to a professional athlete, the real reward at the end of the game. This time it was even more so.

Anyone who has seen me golf knows I am not a player who disguises his emotions. You don't need the TV commentator to tell you if I am happy or up set with a shot. I'll let you know. That's me, not exactly Mr. Mellow. Yet the first few days home, I found myself spending hours in our backyard just looking at the flowers and the trees, or watching birds through binoculars. I was getting so mellow it was beginning to scare me! "Maybe the chemo went to my brain," I told Toni, joking.

The phone rang regularly with well-wishers, including President Bush and even my PGA competitor Greg Norman. I found out that the Shark has a soft side.

Then one morning while I was getting ready for the day, something happened. I stood in my bedroom praying, wondering in the back of my mind what would happen if I didn't get better. The sun was forcing its way through the blinds when suddenly, a powerful feeling swelled over me like a huge, gently rolling wave lifting my feet off the sand bottom of the sea. I stopped everything I was doing and experienced an incredible, peace-giving sensation. I knew that God was with me, and I felt absolutely assured that I would be okay. It wasn't that God told me what would happen next or that the cancer would go away. I simply felt positive I was in His complete and loving care, no matter what.

I am blessed to say that today, two years after my diagnosis, the cancer is gone. I'm back on the tour trying to shake the rust off my golf game. Dr. Jobe said it was probably a good thing I didn't rush out to California right after the PGA title because at that time, the number of cancer cells in my body might not have been sufficient to show up on a biopsy. I guess in a way, my competitive drive saved my life after all, but what keeps me going most these days is the chance to be an example for others who are struck by the disease, to help them see that God is there for them no matter what. That's all you need to know to get through anything in life. That is the real "major."

Which is not to say, of course, that the next time I find myself in a playoff with the Shark you won't be able to tell how I feel about a shot. I am the way God made me, and I don't think the Lord is interested in tinkering with my golf game.

Chapter 3 Healing Hands

When Jesus had entered Capernaum, a centurion came to him, asking for help. "Lord," he said, "my servant lies at home paralyzed and in terrible suffering."

Jesus said to him, "I will go and heal him."

The centurion replied, "Lord, I do not deserve to have you come under my roof. But just say the word, and my servant will be healed. For I myself am a man under authority, with soldiers under me. I tell this one, 'Go,' and he goes; and that one, 'Come,' and he comes. I say to my servant, 'Do this,' and he does it."

When Jesus heard this, he was astonished and said to those following him, "I tell you the truth, I have not found anyone in Israel with such great faith." . . .

Then Jesus said to the centurion, "Go! It will be done just as you believed it would." . . . And his servant was healed at that very hour (Matthew 8:5-10, 13, NIV).

Sometimes we simply need an advocate—someone who will come alongside of us and ask for those things that we cannot ask for ourselves. And healing is one of those things that involve more than just those who are in need of healing. When we are sick or injured, we need help getting medical attention, with our meals and daily needs, with simply maneuvering through life.

In the Gospels we read remarkable stories about the healings of Jesus. Playing supporting roles in many of these stories are people who assisted those who needed healing, either carrying the sick to Jesus or pleading with Jesus to come to the sick. Remember the four men who lowered their lame friend through a roof into a house where Jesus was teaching? Or the mother who sought healing for her daughter, or Jarius who pleaded with Jesus to heal his daughter? Or Peter who asked Jesus to heal his mother-in-law?

The story of the centurion who seeks out Jesus and begs him to heal his servant is remarkable in that this Roman understands what others do not: that the power and authority of Jesus' works derive from the Holy God of the Universe. It is this power and this authority that intervenes in the disease and injuries that we suffer to restore us to health.

We too are often privileged to participate in another person's encounter with a healing God. Sometimes we participate by reaching out to a stranger, sometimes by embracing a loved one. But we must never forget that someone else's healing may depend on our own sensitivity and obedience to the leading of God. Perhaps the words of Simone Weil express this best: "God is present at the point where the eyes of those who give and those who receive meet."

Christ has no body now on earth but yours, no hands but yours, no feet but yours; yours are the eyes through which to look at Christ's compassion to the world, yours are the feet with which He is to go about doing good, and yours are the hands with which He is to bless us now.

—St. Teresa of Avila

"YOU ARE MY SUNSHINE"

YITTA HALBERSTAM AND JUDITH LEVENTHAL

When Karen found out that another baby was on the way, she did what she could to help her three-year-old son Michael prepare for the new sibling. Karen knew she was having a girl, and she spoke to her son often about the upcoming birth. Michael awaited it with eager anticipation. Day after day and night after night, Michael sang to his sister in Mommy's tummy. He was building a bond of love with his little sister before he even met her.

The pregnancy progressed normally for Karen. In time, the labor pains came. Soon they were coming every five minutes. Then every three, every two, and finally every minute. Karen was rushed to the delivery room, and there some serious complications set in. Karen was told that a C-section might very well be required. Finally, Michael's little sister was born.

There was intense joy and reverence at the moment of birth, but the joy quickly gave way to grave concern. The little baby was in serious condition. With a siren howling in the night, the ambulance rushed the infant to the neonatal intensive care unit at St. Mary's Hospital in Knoxville, Tennessee. The pediatric medical team there began working immediately on the baby, but it seemed she would need an enormous amount of care over the next few weeks if she were to stand a fighting chance.

The days inched by with the newborn quite a distance from home. To make matters worse, the little girl's condition seemed to be getting graver as time wore on. "There is very little hope," said the pediatric specialist. "Be prepared for the worst." With deep pain and sorrow, Karen and her husband contacted a local cemetery about a burial plot. They had fixed up a special room in their home for the new baby, but now it seemed that they were going to plan a funeral instead.

Michael, however, kept begging his parents to let him see his sister. "I want to sing to her," he kept saying. As week two in intensive care began, it looked as if a funeral would come before the week was over. Michael kept nagging about singing to his sister, but kids are never allowed in intensive care. But Karen made up her mind: She would take Michael in whether they liked it or not! If he didn't see his sister then, he might never have a chance to see her alive.

She dressed him in an oversized scrub suit and marched him into the ICU. He looked like a walking laundry basket. But the head nurse recognized him as a child and bellowed, "Get that kid out of here now! No children are allowed!" Maternal rage rose up strong in Karen, and the usually mild-mannered woman glared steely-eyed right into the nurse's face, her lips a firm line. "He is not leaving until he sings to his sister!"

Karen towed Michael to his sister's bedside. He gazed at the tiny infant losing her battle to live. After a moment, he began to sing. In the pure-hearted voice of a three-year-old, Michael sang: "You are my sunshine, my only sunshine, you make me happy when skies are gray." Instantly the baby girl seemed to respond. Her pulse rate began to calm down and became steady. "Keep on singing, Michael," encouraged Karen with tears in her eyes.

"You'll never know, dear, how much I love you, please don't take my sunshine away." As Michael sang to his sister, the baby's ragged, strained breathing became as smooth as a kitten's purr.

"Keep on singing, sweetheart!" Karen encouraged.

"The other night, dear, as I lay sleeping, I dreamed I held you in my arms," he sang.

Michael's little sister began to relax, as rest, healing rest, seemed to sweep over her. "Keep on singing, Michael." Tears had now conquered the face of the bossy head nurse. Karen glowed.

"You are my sunshine, my only sunshine. Please don't take my sunshine away," the little boy's voice rang out.

The next day . . . the very next day . . . the little girl was well enough to go home! *Woman's Day* magazine called it "The Miracle of a Brother's Song." The medical staff just called it a miracle. Karen called it a miracle of God's love.

ANGEL IN A DIFFERENT PEW

EVA UNGA

On Sunday mornings in church, Mary Ryerson loves the moment when the choir begins to sing and her young children settle into the pew by her side. *I'm so blessed,* she thinks.

But once in a while, her eyes search out an empty pew in the back—as if to look for the stranger who once sat there, a stranger who saved her family from unthinkable grief . . . .

Mary and her husband Loren were overjoyed when she gave birth to little Michael in 1991. After two miscarriages, the couple finally had a little brother for their nine-year-old son, also named Loren.

"He's perfect!" Mary smiled as she held him for the first time.

"Yep—even if he did get the Ryerson head," her husband said as they fit the blue stocking cap nurses gave them over Michael's head—which filled the cap completely.

"Just like you and Loren," Mary grinned. She'd always had trouble finding hats big enough for her husband.

Still, as Michael grew those first few weeks, his longish head nagged at her.

"He's doing great," her pediatrician said. Still Mary noticed he spent extra time checking for the soft spot on Michael's head at his three-month checkup. "His head is big—I'd like you to take him in for X-rays to make sure it's developing normally," he frowned.

Her heart pounding, Mary raced to the hospital. But hours later, the radiologist told her, "Everything's fine."

"Thank God!" Mary cried, relief washing over her.

Her worries were forgotten a few weeks later as she drove to church, with four-month-old Michael gurgling in his car seat as big brother Loren dangled plastic keys to keep him amused.

When they entered the church, Mary headed for the spot she always sat in, on the right side in the second pew from the front. But she found herself pausing halfway, then noticing a seat in the back on the left-hand side.

"Why don't we sit back there?" she asked.

Loren looked surprised. It was the first time in years they'd sat anywhere other than their usual seats. But he just shrugged and followed his mom to the back.

As she settled the boys into the pew, Mary sensed someone staring at her. Looking up, she saw a man nearby looking intently at her. The congregation was small, but Mary had never seen him before. *I wonder who he is?* she thought, and smiled at him.

Then, at the "handshake of peace," when parishioners stand to shake hands with one another, the man reached right over others to shake her hand. "Peace be with you," he said softly, holding on to her hand longer than was normal. *He wants to say something,* Mary realized. But the man hesitated, then let go and sat back down.

When the service was over, Mary glanced at her watch—she was late for a youth league soccer meeting. She was hurrying out with the children when she heard a voice.

"Excuse me," a man called. "May I speak with you?"

Turning, Mary saw the man who'd been looking at her.

"I don't want to intrude," he began, reaching out and gently touching Michael's head. Usually Michael was fussy with strangers, but with this man, he just cooed.

"Have you taken your baby to a doctor?" the man asked quietly.

"Yes," Mary replied. "He's fine."

"No, he's not," the man said gently. "He has sagital cranial synostosis."

"What?" Mary gasped.

"It's a condition where the plates in the head prematurely fuse together," the man explained. "I suggest you consult a pediatric neurosurgeon immediately."

"But—but—," Mary stammered. "How do you know?"

"I'm a pediatric neurosurgeon visiting from Ohio," the man replied. "Your son needs help."

Mary's stomach fell. "The doctor will explain everything," the man was saying. "But you have to get there soon."

By now, churchgoers were streaming out the door and all around them. "Thank you," Mary managed to stammer before the man disappeared into the crowd.

Alarmed, she called her pediatrician, who gave her the name of a doctor in Denver. "But it's almost impossible to get an appointment with him—you may have to wait," the pediatrician warned.

But we can't! Mary thought, alarmed.

And incredibly, she didn't have to. "We just had a cancellation—the call before you," the doctor's office told her when she phoned.

In Denver, a pediatric neurosurgeon confirmed the stranger's diagnosis. The four plates in Michael's head had already fused together. "There's no place for his brain to grow," the surgeon explained. Without surgery, Michael would become permanently brain-damaged.

"Luckily, he's young so his skull is still soft enough to operate on," the surgeon added. "You brought him in just in time."

Mary felt tingles go down her spine as she recalled the man in church *He knew!* she realized, amazed. *Oh, how I wish I had asked his name!*

A few weeks later, Mary and Loren watched as little Michael was prepped for surgery. A team of doctors would remove his skull, cut it into pieces and reassemble it with wires, giving his brain room to grow. It was a terrifying prospect—but it was her baby's only hope.

In the waiting room, the hours dragged on endlessly. Mary couldn't concentrate on the magazines; exhausted, she couldn't sleep. At last, eight and a half hours later: "It went beautifully!" the surgeon announced. "Michael's going to be just fine."

"Oh, thank you!" Mary gasped through tears of joy.

Four days later, Michael was released. Though he had to wear a helmet for a year to protect his head, he healed completely. And as he grew—chasing butterflies in the garden, pleading for a Popsicle at the sound of the ice cream truck—Mary could only watch in wonder. *He is perfect,* she thought.

Today, when Mary watches six-year-old Michael play street hockey or ride his bike with the neighborhood kids, she thinks about that fateful day in church when a stranger cared enough to stop.

"Who knows what Michael's life would be like if we had sat in our usual seat?" she smiles. "We might never have shaken hands with our guardian angel."

ERIN'S CHRISTMAS VISION

Joan Wester Anderson

Kathy and Mike Felke, of northwest suburban Illinois, were thrilled at the birth of their second daughter, Erin, in 1978. But unlike her older sister, Kate, Erin seemed fragile. Although she walked early, she preferred being carried.

"Everyone thought she was an exceptionally good baby because she always sat in my lap, and she slept a lot," says Kathy, a registered dental hygienist. "Actually, she caught every illness that came around, especially ear infections. I knew enough about health to realize something was wrong."

Kathy and Mike repeatedly mentioned their concern about Erin to their pediatrician. But blood tests showed nothing. Finally the doctor told Kathy that she was just "an overly concerned mother."

On December 23, 1980, two-year-old Erin seemed unusually listless. She barely ate breakfast, then fell asleep on the couch. Kathy looked at her. "I could almost see the veins under her skin," she says, "and the shadows around her eyes were as dark as her hair." Kathy phoned her pediatrician's partner, and insisted on an immediate appointment.

The new doctor checked Erin. "How long has she looked like this?" he asked abruptly.

Kathy thought. "Over a year. But tests haven't shown anything."

"I want a complete blood workup at the hospital," he said, reaching for the phone. "Bring her there right now."

Kathy did. The following morning, Christmas Eve, the physician phoned. "I have some bad news," he told her. "Erin is gravely ill. It might be aplastic anemia or leukemia."

Kathy's heart seemed to stop.

"I've arranged for a private room at Loyola Medical Center," the doctor went on. "The chief of hematology there will take over Erin's treatment. You can take her in early on the twenty-sixth."

He stopped, then sighed. "She might as well spend Christmas at home."

Kathy didn't miss the tinge of hopelessness in his voice. Devastated, she told Mike, then began phoning family members.

The following morning, Kathy bravely dressed Erin in her red jumper, onto which Erin's grandmother pinned a gold angel pin. They drove to Holy Ghost Parish in Wood Dale, and went to the sanctuary where Father Tom White was vesting, to tell him what had happened.

Father White listened. He blessed Erin, and added her name to the list of ill parishioners who would be prayed for during Christmas mass. And, although the

Felkes hadn't realized it yet, he threw away his prepared homily. "I do that a lot," Father White says today. "Sometimes everything I planned to say will change in an instant."

A few moments later, Father White stood in front of a packed church. Looking down, he saw Erin in the front row, drowsing on Kathy's lap.

"Life isn't easy," he began. "Sometimes we're presented with things we can't accept, situations too big even to comprehend. And we get mad at God about it." He began to pace back and forth in front of the congregation. "During those times, God understands how we feel—and it's okay to be angry with Him. But we also have to remember that we don't need just to lie down and take it."

Father White looked at the Felkes in the first row. "No—when we're presented with heartbreak, He wants us to *fight*! We have to use the faith we've been given!"

On the way home from church Kathy and Mike agreed that the priest had given them hope. Tomorrow the battle would begin.

The next morning, Kathy packed Erin's crib sheet, potty chair, and special dish, and drawings from Kate to hang near her bed. "Maybe I was in denial, but I wanted everything to be as normal as possible," she says. A team of physicians met them at the hospital, and when they found that Erin's hemoglobin had sunk to 4.5 (a normal reading is between eleven and fifteen), the pace quickened. A bone marrow test revealed that Erin's body was making red cells, yet something was destroying them almost immediately. But what?

Kathy and Mike gave extensive family histories. Their use of pesticides, their allergies, antibiotics combating Erin's constant ear infections—specialists examined everything for clues. And everything led to a dead end. Three days later there was still no diagnosis, no recommended treatment.

Kathy refused to go home, so nurses brought a bed for her. "At one point a nurse told me that a prayer group had assembled in the playroom, and wanted to see me," she said. Kathy went out to meet them. "They said they had heard about Erin, and had come to pray for her, but they didn't introduce themselves, and I had never seen any of them before." The group knelt in a circle, with Kathy in their midst, and prayed strongly for healing. They were fighting, Kathy realized, fighting for a toddler they had never met. But being away from Erin upset her, and she didn't stay long. The next time she left Erin's side, the group had gone.

By the evening of the twenty-eighth, Erin was sleeping almost constantly. When the doctor came, he shook his head. "You'd better prepare yourself," he told Kathy gently. "We're losing her. The only possibility left is a blood transfusion, to keep her alive a little longer. But we can't find a compatible donor right now."

"Take mine!" But Kathy already knew she wasn't a match.

"Look, Mrs. Felke," the doctor continued, "Erin's oxygen level is falling. So I think you need to face—"

"No!" She couldn't! The doctor quietly left. At midnight a priest appeared, prayed over Erin, and anointed her. They were all fighting for Erin, Kathy realized: Mike, at home with Kate, Father White, the hospital staff, all the people who were praying. She might be lonely, but she and Erin were not alone. Intently she watched her daughter. *Fight, Erin, fight.* Every breath, every heartbeat, was a small victory.

But Erin's skin was almost transparent now, her eyes ringed with shadows. A haze seemed to be lying over her, as if life were ebbing away, growing fainter, foggier . . .

Suddenly, at 1:30 A.M., Erin opened her eyes. She looked aware, present. Kathy was astonished. "Lights, Mommy. Lights!" Erin whispered, her gaze fixed on something above Kathy's head. Kathy turned, but saw nothing in the darkened room.

"Where are the lights, honey?" she whispered, turning back. "What do you see?"

Erin looked thrilled. "Bells, Mommy!" she cried, her voice slightly stronger. "Lights and bells!"

The hospital corridors were completely hushed. Kathy's skin prickled. What could Erin be hearing? Was she hallucinating? No, she seemed extremely alert.

Now Erin smiled. Raising a tiny hand, she pointed to the corner of the room. "Pretty ladies, Mommy. See them?" On her face was an expression of joy.

Pretty ladies . . . Kathy was afraid to turn around. What would she see? She had heard that angels came to carry people home to heaven. Was that what was happening? Was Erin seeing angels?

No! Suddenly Kathy's heart seemed to break. She hadn't fought yet, she realized—others had been doing it for her. But now it was her turn! *Oh, God, angels, don't take her!* she prayed silently. *Take me—not her. She hasn't even started to live. Please, please.*

A nurse came into the room. "We've found a reasonable blood match," she told Kathy. "We're going to start a very slow transfusion. You'll have to watch each drop, in case it begins to clot."

Kathy looked back at Erin. Her daughter's eyes were closing again. But a smile remained on her lips.

Kathy stayed alert for the rest of the night, watching the miniature droplets inch down the tube, and into her daughter. Would the transfusion work? If not, Kathy knew, there were no other options.

Mike came in early that morning, while Erin was still sleeping. So he, too, witnessed the beginning of the miracle. "She awakened, and we both just stared at her," Kathy says. There was color in her daughter's lips. Erin's cheeks were pink, not gray.

"Do you feel like breakfast?" Kathy asked.

Erin nodded.

By evening, her hemoglobin had mysteriously increased to a reading of 8. "We don't know what has happened," her physician told the Felkes. "But the transfusion must have worked, because Erin seems fine. She might as well go home now."

Erin remained healthy. Now an active teenager, she has a complete blood workup every year, but no problem has surfaced. But because Erin left the hospital with her condition described as "undiagnosed," Kathy and Mike were not aware of the full extent of what had happened until several years later.

"When we moved and changed doctors, I brought Erin's records to our new pediatrician," Kathy says. "He was interested, and did some research." Only then did she learn, says Kathy, that Erin's disease was a rare form of anemia, one that at that time had proved fatal to six of the only seven Americans who'd been diagnosed with it. There had been no treatment then, and although blood transfusions had been tried in other cases, they had never worked.

Kathy's learned much from this difficult episode, especially about God and the power of prayer. "I don't know why He healed Erin, and not another child whose parents loved her just as much and prayed just as hard," she says. "But I know now that it's okay to be mad at Him. He doesn't hold grudges, and He does understand." And when His light breaks through our darkness, Kathy knows it can conquer even death itself.

THE MESSAGE

GINGER DAVIS GETTLE

'm going to die, aren't I?" I said to my husband. "Tell me!"

Bob pulled his chair close to my hospital bed and took my hand. "You have to have another operation," he said, "maybe two. The tests taken after your stroke show you have two weak spots in the arteries in your brain. If they're not repaired, you'll have another stroke." He didn't add, "...and *that* stroke will be fatal," but I knew that's what he meant.

I pulled my hand away. "How much will it cost?"

His voice sank to a whisper. "About two hundred and fifty thousand dollars," he said, "...or more."

I closed my eyes and sank back against my pillow. Two hundred and fifty thousand dollars—when we barely had enough to pay the grocery bills. And even if we had the money, I was so traumatized by just the thought of surgery that I couldn't imagine going through it. Plus I had a history of health problems—ulcers, allergic reactions, unusual complications after other medical procedures—that didn't bode well for *any* operation, much less highly complicated ones.

"What happens if I don't have the surgery, Bob?" I asked, "I'll die, won't I?" Bob didn't answer. Instead he moved onto the edge of my bed and put his arms around me. But I barely felt them. *This is it,* I thought. *The end of my life.* And the end of a year filled with one devastating event after another.

The past year in Houston had been terrible for us. Oil prices had plunged and Bob had been laid off from his job on an offshore oil rig. He'd been looking for work steadily, but nothing had come up. In the meantime his unemployment checks had stopped and our savings had dwindled away.

Next came the news that Bob's mother had Alzheimer's disease and his father had a malignant tumor. Bob and I moved in with Mom and Pop to care for them. Foolish as it was, we put off getting health insurance; we didn't have a cent to spare, and Bob would be getting a job any day now . . . or so we thought.

I too was in a downward spiral of sinking spirits and increasing health problems. And then this! When I awoke one morning in late November my right leg and arm were strangely "asleep," and my mouth couldn't form the words I wanted to say. I managed to throw myself out of bed and into the hall, but then I collapsed. I was rushed to the hospital.

For two weeks I couldn't talk or communicate. I had never been so frightened. I went through a series of exhausting tests—and now Bob was at my side telling me the results:

Without the money, no operation.

Without the operation, no life.

"Then I'll just die," I said.

His arms tightened around me. But I pulled away. As much as I loved him, I wanted him to leave. "Go home," I said. "You need the rest." Inside of me the message was different: *I'm going to die. Go away. Leave me alone.*

Slowly he pulled on his jacket. After he left, the room was silent. *Thank goodness the other bed is empty,* I thought. I couldn't stand to have anybody else near me.

There was the squish of rubber-soled shoes in the corridor. I turned my head to see a wheelchair roll in, pushed by a smiling nurse. "Good news, Mrs. Gettle. You're getting company," she said.

A roommate! That was all I needed. I watched grudgingly as a slender black woman was helped out of the chair and into the adjoining bed. She had a pleasant face framed by soft gray hair. "Hello," she said, looking over as the nurse adjusted her covers. "I'm Flossie."

"Hello," I said wearily.

"What are you here for?" Flossie's voice was warm and friendly, but I was in no mood for talking. Tersely I explained my physical condition.

"When are they going to fix you up?" Flossie asked.

Never, I thought to myself, choking back tears. "There are some problems,"

I said. "We can't afford the surgery." As the nurse turned to go, I asked her to pull the curtains around my bed. "I'd like some privacy," I said weakly.

The curtains rattled on their rod, then closed around me like a tent, and Flossie vanished out of sight behind them. Vaguely I heard some muffled conversation about a mysterious attack that Flossie had had that evening. Her husband had rushed her to the hospital, and she was being kept overnight for observation.

But I paid little attention to what was going on. I curled up in misery.

I'd always been a "Christian" person. My mother had been a minister, and I had gone through all the right motions and participated in all the right church activities. But what good had it all done?

I felt totally abandoned. How would my husband cope when I was gone? Who would take care of Mom and Pop? Fears swirled in terrifying profusion. You'll die, you'll die, with every breath I took. You'll die, you'll die, you'll die . . . .

The words sounded in my mind, with every breath I took. You'll die, you'll die, you'll die . . . .

I fell into a heavy, churning sleep . . . .

"Mrs. Gettle, wake up!" A voice called me; a hand was shaking my shoulder gently but firmly. The curtains that shrouded my bed had parted; a form leaned over me, silhouetted against the eerie glow of a small night-light in the corridor outside.

"What's wrong?" I mumbled.

"Nothing's wrong, honey," said a rich, gentle voice. "I have a message for you. From God."

From God? Flossie?

It *was* Flossie. She had left her own bed and was standing next to mine.

"I've been praying about you," she said, "and God spoke to me clear as a bell. He said, 'Tell this lady I'm going to give her her surgery, and it's going to be successful.' She patted my hand. "Now don't you worry about another thing. You'll *live*."

With a tremble of the curtains, she was gone. I lay staring at the glowing hall light. The small clock on my bedside table said it was 2:30 in the morning, the middle of the night.

Abruptly I was filled with an overwhelming sense of peace. It was as if gentle hands had grasped my shoulders and turned me completely around. The hammering, negative voice in my head stopped. It was replaced with a fresher, calmer cadence. *You'll live, you'll live, you'll live . . .* I drifted back to sleep and slept better than I had in months.

The next morning I was released from the hospital. I was told that, short of having the necessary surgery, nothing further could be done for me. As I packed my things to go home, Flossie smiled knowingly from the next bed. "It will be all right, honey," she said with such conviction that it was impossible to doubt her. "God told me so."

Bob looked at me strangely as he drove me home. "It's good to see you so cheerful," he said. "Especially since you don't feel well."

Don't feel well? After months of illness and depression, I was feeling better and better. Instead of slumping down onto my bed the way I might have a few days before, I had the urge to get busy in the house, maybe even to check in with the neighbors to see what had happened since I'd been away.

You'll live. God will give you the surgery.

I saw my neighbor's car pass the window and pull into the driveway next door.

My neighbor, Dr. Howard Derman—I'd said hello to him over the fence, but that was all. But suddenly it hit me that he was a neurologist. He'd know more about what they told me in the hospital. I was out the door before my astonished husband could ask where I was going.

Dr. Derman was at his kitchen table having breakfast. I told him about my diagnosis and asked him to explain.

He drew on the napkin to illustrate. "There are two weak places in your arteries that bulge out," he explained. "If they aren't repaired, they can blow out, just like a weak spot on a tire." He went into more detail about the surgery, then asked who would be doing it.

"No one," I said. "We can't afford it."

He looked thoughtful for a moment, then began asking questions about Bob and me and our finances. "I'm affiliated with a local hospital," he said. On a previous visit there I'd been told I wasn't "destitute enough" to qualify for special assistance. "It just seems to me," he went on, "that if ever two people needed special funding, it's you and Bob. Let me see what I can do."

It's hard to believe what happened next. Since my case was so unusual, the doctors asked if my operation could be filmed for teaching and research purposes, and the hospital would pay all charges. Is that what Flossie's incredible statement meant: "Tell this lady I'm going to *give* her the surgery?"

Bob couldn't get over how calm I was as they rolled me down toward the operating room, clutching a piece of paper bearing the words, *Let not your heart be troubled* (John 14:1, KJV).

I went through nearly nine hours of complicated surgery to repair the first aneurysm—and it all went smoothly. Within a few days I was up and walking in the halls. The doctors were amazed at my quick recovery. Ordinarily they would have sent me home for a few months to recover and regain my strength for the second operation, but I felt so strong and confident that I said, "Let's go ahead now."

Only thirteen days later I had another operation—and four days after that I was out of intensive care and walking around the wards, helping the nurses with some of their duties. No more lying around thinking about dying for me! The hospital staff could hardly believe it. When they commented on how well I was coping, I gave the explanation I'd given from the first.

"Oh," they said, laughing, "you're back to 'God gave me the surgery,' are you?"

But I could tell they were impressed.

What turned me around—from a timid, fear-filled person to a confident, lively one? A lot of people would say it was the power of suggestion and I agree: God's suggestion, passed on by one of His faithful messengers and given to a desperate woman deep in despair in the middle of the night. How did that messenger happen to be in the bed next to mine that fateful night? That's one of the mysteries, for the doctors never found anything wrong with Flossie. She went home fine, and has stayed fine. I know, because Flossie and I have been fast friends ever since.

"When I woke you up that night," Flossie once said, "you must have wondered, 'What on earth's got into her?'"

And then she and I laughed, because we knew. It was nothing on earth.

Nothing on earth at all.

IMMY'S MEDAL

RACHEL NAOMI REMEN, M.D.

mmy was a frail little girl, the only child of older parents. At three, she was only as big as the average eighteen-month-old toddler. She was unable to walk more than a few blocks without tiring and did not have the strength to play games you could not play sitting down. A desperately wanted and long-awaited baby, she had been born with a hole in her heart and a badly formed heart valve. Only the most careful medical management had helped her to live until she was big enough to undergo extensive open-heart surgery. She had been followed since birth in our Pediatric Cardiology Clinic at New York Hospital, and many of the pediatricians knew her and her family. Despite her physical difficulties, she took full possession of all the hearts around her, including mine.

When the time for her surgery finally came, her parents were deeply anxious. These were the early days for many cardiac surgery techniques, and the risks were considerable, but without surgery she would not survive childhood. As the senior pediatric resident, I met with Immy's parents before the surgery to do an intake interview and summarize Immy's long story. They were committed and ready and very pale. As we spoke, they sat close together holding hands. Afterward, I took them with me to the children's ward to examine Immy. She greeted us with her take-no-prisoners smile. She was holding a new teddy bear. Someone had put a white bandage across its chest.

I examined Immy carefully. Her heart sounds bore no resemblance whatever to the organized sounds of a normal heart. Once again, I marveled at her endurance. As I helped her to dress, I noticed a St. Christopher medal pinned to her tiny pink undershirt. "What is this?" I asked her parents. Hesitantly, her mother told me that a family member had made a special trip to Rome to have the medal blessed and then dipped into the healing water at Lourdes. "We feel that it will protect her," she said simply. Her husband nodded. I was touched.

Immy spent the next day or two undergoing tests, and I saw her several more times. The medal had been moved from her shirt to her hospital gown. It had seemed so important to her parents that I mentioned it in passing to the cardiac surgery resident as we sat writing chart notes in the nursing station on the evening before the surgery. He gave me a cynical smile. "Well, to each his own," he said. "I put my faith in Dr. X," he said, mentioning the name of the highly respected cardiac surgeon who would be heading Immy's surgical team in the morning. "I doubt he needs much help from Lourdes."

I made a note to myself to be sure to take the medal off Immy's gown before she went to surgery in the morning so it wouldn't get lost in the operating room or the recovery room. But I spent that morning in the emergency room as part of a team working on two children who had been thrown from the back of their father's pick-up truck onto the roadway. By the time I reached the floor, Immy had been taken upstairs to surgery.

Immy's mother told me in a shaking voice that the medal was gone. "Perhaps you should tell the surgeon," I told the surgery resident. He began to laugh. "Don't be absurd," he said.

The surgery lasted almost twelve hours, and things had not gone well. The bypass pump, a relatively new technology, had malfunctioned for several minutes, and Immy had lost a great deal of blood. She was on a respirator, unconscious and unresponsive, in the intensive care unit.

On the day after the surgery, Immy's mother told me in a shaking voice that Immy's gown had been removed in the operating room and thrown into the hospital laundry. The medal was gone. Concerned, I called the surgery resident and told him what had happened.

"Perhaps you should tell Dr. X," I told him. He began to laugh.

"Don't be absurd," he said.

That night, I could not sleep. Back in the house-staff residence, I kept thinking of the lost medal and what Immy's parents had told me. At last, sometime after 2:00 A.M., I took some paper and wrote a note to Dr. X, telling him what had happened and how important the medal was to Immy's family. Folding the note in half, I dressed and went back to the hospital to tape it to the closed door of Dr. X's office. I had signed it, and on my way back to bed I began to worry. What if I had done something really foolish? If the surgical resident didn't care about such things, why should Dr. X?

When I returned to the hospital for the evening shift, I stopped by the intensive care unit to examine Immy and speak with her family. She was still unconscious. Leaning over to listen to her chest, I suddenly noticed a medal pinned to her hospital gown. Turning to her parents in relief, I asked if it was another one. "No," her mother said, "it is the same one that was lost." Dr. X had come that afternoon and brought it to them. I told them how glad I was that it had been found. "Yes," her father said, "we are too." Then he smiled. "She is safe now, no matter what happens."

The following morning, the surgery resident told me how the medal had been found. On the previous day, Dr. X had made his patient-care rounds much as usual, followed by a dozen of the young surgeons he was training. But instead of ending the rounds in the ICU, he had taken them all to the laundry department in the subbasement of the hospital. There, he explained what had happened, and then he and all his residents and fellows had gone through the pediatric laundry from the day before looking for Immy's gown. It had taken half an hour, but they had found it, neatly folded, with the medal still attached.

I was astonished. "Did he say why he asked you to do this?"

"Oh, yes," the resident replied. Surrounded by mountains of clean sheets and towels, Dr. X had told the elite young surgeons he was training that it was as important to care for people's souls as it was to care for their hearts.

HEAVEN IN HAZARD

JOAN WESTER ANDERSON

Ken Gaub grew up in Yakima, Washington, the oldest of six and the son of a man who at one time had no use for God. But over the years, Ken's parents developed a deep spiritual faith. "I began to see amazing miracles and answers to prayer in my parents' lives," Ken says, "and I knew it had to be because of their commitment to God." And that was fine.

But not for Ken. Oh, he had nothing against religion or the ministry. At times he'd even practiced preaching—"I'd get wound up and do a lot of hellfire and brimstone"—but Ken also had a gift for making people laugh. He was the life of the party and hoped someday to be a professional comedian. He didn't see how both vocations could exist side by side. By the time Ken reached his teens, he was also somewhat of a daredevil who enjoyed taking risks. But God seemed to protect him anyway.

For example, Ken had fixed up an old car and took it out for a test-drive one afternoon. Faster and faster he went down a deserted road. The gas pedal was almost to the floor when Ken spotted a large cardboard box lying ahead of him in the middle of the road. He would hit it and watch it explode all over the place!

"But just before I reached it, I felt the steering wheel turning," Ken recalls. "The car was being taken out of my control, and somehow it went completely around the box without touching it at all." Shocked, Ken looked in the rearview mirror and broke out in a cold sweat. Two little children were getting out of the box.

Ken knew that God had intervened in this situation. He was grateful but still not convinced that he was being called to the religious life. One night, however, Ken's father took the family to see a traveling minister conduct a religious revival in a tent. More than ten thousand people attended, and Ken was spellbound as miracle after miracle took place. On the way home, he announced to his parents, "Someday I'm going to do like that preacher. I'm going to have a tent and preach, and I'm going to help people just as he did."

It was certainly a worthy goal, but many years passed—and a lot of hardship and backsliding—before Ken began to see the beginnings of his dreams come true. He met his wife, Barbara, at Bible college in Washington, married her shortly before graduation and decided they should leave for Kentucky. "Kentucky?" Barbara asked him. "Why there?"

Ken knew nothing about Kentucky except what he had seen illustrated in books. But his father had once lived there and had often described its beautiful mountains and creeks. "I think a lot of people need us there," Ken told her, so they loaded their old car with everything they owned and set out on their three-thousand-mile journey.

The couple evangelized their way across the country, "but either the people in those cities went to bed real early or had other things to do," Ken says, because their turnouts were small. What if they got to Kentucky and discovered that this was *not* the place God intended them to go?

But once the Gaubs arrived, they discovered that although the people were poor, they were also hungry for education. After Ken and Barbara found a place to live and a place to conduct worship, the neighbors came from everywhere around Hazard to attend, sometimes walking for miles, barefoot despite the danger of snakes. Ken spent hours visiting up and down their creek dwellings and started a Bible school for the children. Money was always short, and Ken and Barbara lived on the edge most of the time, but God helped too. One day Ken had only one dollar to use for gasoline for his car. The attendant put in the dollar's worth, but when Ken pulled away, his tank was completely full. On other occasions, just as they spent the last of their money on food, someone would bring them something to eat. "We simply tried to obey the Lord and bless other people," Ken explains. "The more we blessed them, the more they blessed us."

But of course there were also people, as in any mission field, whose hearts were closed to the word of God. Ken usually respected their beliefs. And yet if someone in an unbelieving family was sick, it was hard for Ken not to visit, since praying for healing was, to him, one of the most important parts of his work. One day he met

Millie Johnson* downtown. Millie's husband, Jake, a giant of a man, had told Ken in no uncertain terms several times just what he would do to him if he talked "that religion stuff" with Millie. But now Millie approached Ken with tears in her eyes. "Jeremy's very sick, Preacher," she said. "He's in the hospital." Jeremy was the Johnsons' year-old baby. "Do you think you could go and pray for him?"

"Millie, I'd be happy to go," Ken told her. "But you know how Jake feels about it."

"He's on a trip today," Millie said. "He'll never know."

"Okay," Ken had been heading to the hospital anyway, so he took some extra time to stop in Jeremy's room, lay hands on the baby and pray for his recovery.

For the week, each time he made his hospital rounds, Ken kept a lookout for Jake. If the man was visiting with his son, Ken bypassed the baby's room. If he saw Jake leaving, he knew he could stop to pray.

One particular day, the hallway outside Jeremy's room seemed exceptionally quiet. Ken peeked in. No one was in the room, so he tiptoed over to the crib where the baby lay with a sheet on top of him. Reaching out his hand, he softly touched the sheet covering Jeremy so as not to awaken him. "Lord," he prayed, "raise up this baby for Your glory."

---

*Name has been changed.

Uh-oh. The baby had started squirming. Ken thought he had better get out of there before Jeremy cried and attracted attention. Just as Ken turned to leave, he saw that the doorway was blocked by Jake's very large frame. Jake was glaring at Ken.

"Now, Jake . . ." Ken began.

Then Jake looked over at the crib, and saw the sheet moving. "Oh, God! Oh, God!" he cried.

Ken tried to think of something to say to placate him and get around him. By now, Jake's yelling had attracted a nurse. "Please, sir, this is a hospital," she said to Jake. "Calm down. I realize this is hard on you, but . . ."

Jake continued to yell and point at the crib. Then the nurse looked at the crib, and she screamed. All the color faded from her face as she backed out the door and ran down the corridor. Jake ran over and picked up the child.

Ken was at a loss as to why everyone was so upset. Maybe the baby was dying. Obviously, Ken had made the situation worse, so he left quickly, before anything else could happen.

When the hospital phoned later to say that the parents wanted Ken to return, he assumed that little Jeremy had died—either that, or Ken was going to be reprimanded for intruding. Not knowing what to expect, he was flabbergasted when Jake rushed up and threw his arms around him. "Preacher, I want you to know that I changed my mind about that religious stuff. I believe now!" He began weeping again and couldn't say any more.

"What's going on?" Ken asked.

Millie looked at him, tears streaming down her cheeks. "Preacher, didn't you know that our Jeremy had died two hours before you prayed for him?"

"What?" Ken was stunned.

"They had pronounced him dead. They were just waiting for Jake to have a last look at him."

"Well, I didn't know that," Ken explained. "I just felt I had to pray for that baby. I just asked God to raise him up for His glory."

"And God did?" Jake asked.

"We serve a wonderful God, Jake," Ken explained. His heart was full. God had certainly shown him that right here in Hazard, Kentucky, was where He wanted Ken and Barbara to be. And there would be no shortage of signs and wonders, as long as they placed their trust in Him.

Chapter 4 To the Glory of God

esus left there and went along the Sea of Galilee. Then he went up into the hills and sat down. Great crowds came to him, bringing the lame, the blind, the crippled, the mute and many others, and laid them at his feet; and he healed them. The people were amazed when they saw the dumb speaking, the crippled made well, the lame walking and the blind seeing. And they praised the God of Israel (Matthew 15:29-31, NIV).

Have you ever sat in a hospital waiting room, waiting for a surgeon to emerge from the OR with the results of a spouse's bypass surgery? Or waited in the emergency room for the doctors to let you see your child after an auto accident? Or waited for the nurse to call with the results of a biopsy? Life is entirely suspended, as we wait for the word that will reveal the picture of the future.

Then the word comes. "He'll be fine." "The tests are all negative." "She came through with flying colors." Healing is ours. And in one heartbeat, life begins again.

Some shout and hug the doctor. Others collapse and weep with relief. Most of us are overwhelmed by feelings of sheer joy and profound gratitude. When our health restored, all our hopes for the future are also restored. We feel loved, cherished, and protected—and we feel thankful.

Healing is one occasion when God has our complete attention. We are completely focused on the crisis of illness or injury, so that when God intervenes to heal, all of our energy and attention turns to Him, to His work in our lives. It is at the point of our healings that we are connected totally—both physically and spiritually—to the Creator of the Universe.

Like the people of Galilee, we are amazed when the lame walk, the injured are made well and the blind see. Our lives too are touched by God's goodness and by His grace, and we also praise the God of Israel.

When the dawn appears,
When the light grows,
When midday burns,
When has ceased the holy light,
When the clear night comes;
I sing your praises, O Father,

Healer of hearts,
Healer of bodies,
Giver of wisdom,
Remedy of evil.

—Synesius of Cyrene

THE DIVINE TOUCH

MARK BUNTAIN

N ita Edwards was a lovely young Sri Lankan student and athlete who relished her schoolwork as well as tennis, skiing and other sports. Then one day she tumbled down the grand stone staircase at her boarding school, crushing two discs in her lower back, leaving her in excruciating pain and ultimately leading to a paralysis in her legs. As she clung to God's promises for healing, the paralysis spread, eventually encompassing her whole body, head to toe, including her face and scalp. As hours melted into days, days into weeks and weeks into months, Nita struggled not only with the sorrow and frustrations of total physical helplessness, but also with the overwhelming battle to remember God's faithfulness to her in all situations.

Nita lay in her misery for four hours, wide awake, unable to escape into sleep. The soft sounds of the afternoon around her apartment filtered lightly into her room.

Suddenly at about four o'clock she heard a voice behind her. It was the most powerful tone she had ever heard. "Nita, I'm going to raise you up to make you a witness to Asia."

She was startled. If she had been able to, she would have jumped. She had thought she was alone in the room. Where had that voice come from? It said further, "I'm going to heal you on Friday, the eleventh of February."

Nita's heart pounded. She was sure no one was in the room. She had never heard that voice before and felt an uncanny twinge in her spirit.

She struggled for the call button and buzzed for her attendant. If there was a man in the room, she wanted to know. . . . Perhaps under her bed? Nita made the girl get down on her hands and knees and look. No one was there.

Skeptically, but with excitement mounting slowly inside of her, Nita mentally checked off the possibilities. It could have been a dream, but she was wide awake. It could have been a hallucination, but she was not taking medication. It could have been her own imagination, but she wasn't in a good enough frame of mind to think up such a thing. The radio was off and there was no recording equipment around.

Which left two possible sources: God or the devil.

Nita had never taken kindly to people who proclaimed that God had spoken to them. She had always been suspicious of that whole realm of thinking. But deep in her heart, she already knew she had heard from God, that He was going to heal her on Friday, February 11, and that He had answered her prayers in a unique and thoroughly dramatic way.

Still, she just had to be sure.

So she prayed a hard-nosed, practical prayer: "Lord, I've heard this voice. If it's Yours, I want a confirmation."

She felt suddenly awkward, being so bold with the almighty Creator Who had just promised to heal her and done so in an audible voice. But she thought of Gideon laying out his fleece and decided to press on with it.

"I want to hear the promise again," she prayed bravely. "In public. Let other people hear it, too."

She never mentioned the incident to anyone; never hinted that she had heard from God or that she was seeking a confirmation. But she steadily kept her heart open, worshiping her Lord for hours on end, day after day....

One Sunday, Colton, Nita's pastor and faithful prayer supporter, took her to church in a wheelchair. He arranged for them to arrive early, so Nita could be situated in the choir loft between the piano and the wall—neither Colton nor Nita wanted her to be a spectacle. From her cubicle and with her vision problems, she could see very little of what went on, but in the divine plan she was really only there to hear one thing.

It came as a prophetic message, spoken by one of the parishioners. He lifted his voice and declared, "God will raise you up to be a witness to all of Asia. His word to you is true. Trust Him. He will not lead you astray. He will glorify Himself through you."

Nita's heart began to leap with joy. It was true. She had heard from God, and He had confirmed it—here, before fourteen hundred people. The very words that God had said to her.

Nita was ecstatic. Long after the crowd had cleared she was hoisted out of her little hole. And in her heart, she felt that there would be icing on the cake as well: He would speak to her further.

It was in this victorious frame of mind that Nita decided to ask for more information. As the nurse changed her bed linen the next morning, Nita was placed in her wheelchair. She sat by the window with the sunlight streaming in on the pages of her Bible and thought about the day she would be healed.

"Father, You told me the day and the date," she said simply. "Please, don't keep me waiting all day. Please tell me the time too."

She half-expected to hear the voice again, but heard nothing. Instead, a silent inner voice spoke to her spirit: She would be healed at 3:30 in the afternoon.

Nita thought she would burst with excitement. She had the date and the hour now—February 11 at 3:30 P.M. She was going to be healed by the power of God, and she was going to watch it happen.

How she would ever take the Gospel to Asia she had no idea. But of her healing, of the date and the hour, she was utterly sure. God had given her the supernatural gift of faith. In her mind the healing had already happened. All that remained was the gathering of the evidence!

In the past the afternoon sponging had always led to the same thing: The attendant would dress her in clean bed-clothes. But on February 11 Nita had a different idea.

"Bring me my slacks," she said.

As Nita slipped ever nearer to the heart of God, the chosen few she had asked to witness the miracle began to assemble around her.

At two o'clock, Colton and his wife Suzanne arrived, solemn and quiet. They knew this would soon be holy ground. It was clear from the glow on Nita's face the transformation would soon begin. They didn't talk to her at all, but sat down and began to pray quietly. . . .

Two women doctors stepped into the room. They were medical professionals who loved the Lord and who had examined and treated Nita during parts of her long ordeal. They had no hint of what was going to happen here; Colton had only invited them to a special time of prayer. They were honored. They knew Nita Edwards was in seclusion and only a select few had ever been behind these doors. . . .

The room was filled with prayer and a sense of awe, and the supernatural transformation began. The power of God invaded the room, from the right side of her bed, like a ball of fire. The glory of God burst in, flooding that tiny space with such intensity that the inhabitants were swept up in it and overcome by it. It was like looking directly at the noonday sun and only being able to take in a tiny fraction of the radiance.

The air was charged with a fantastic burst of electricity.

Nita felt what seemed like a million volts of power coursing through her body. Every cell, every fiber, every tissue pulsed with it. Wave after wave rolled through her. She was oblivious to her surroundings, to the others. She was longing to see Jesus.

Just at 3:30, He came into the room with blinding glory. Nita gazed into his face, and everything within her struggled to reach out to Him. Her healing was no more a factor. She was unaware of her physical condition. She longed only to touch Him . . . to connect somehow with that fabulous source of light and love.

As she looked at Him, He moved toward her. She was suspended in time and space, filled beyond capacity by the unfathomable love of God. He came to the foot of her bed, and then He reached out with a nail-scarred hand and touched her. One time.

The chains of paralysis exploded away and Nita rocketed out over the end of her bed.

She landed on her knees with a thud, and a first sensation was the cold, hard tile floor beneath her. The divine warmth of the touch of her Lord had suddenly given way to this startling awakening. In the days to come, she would realize that God had touched her so warmly only to thrust her into a ministry of fervent intercessory prayer in the cold, real world.

Her knees had not been bent in over a year; now they were bent before Jesus. Her hands, useless for so long, were now straightened, raised up, worshiping God. Her voice had been still; now her mouth began to fill with heavenly words, tumbling out in a bubbly fountain of praise. For the first time in her life, she was leading others in prayer.

Editor's Note: Nita Edwards traveled throughout Asia for many years, preaching and sharing God's miraculous healing love. Today she continues her work of intercession and teaching through a radio ministry called Asia Alive, based in Annandale, Virginia.

HEALING HANDS

KELSEY TYLER

n 1981, newly married and fresh out of Bible college, Cheri and Ralph Brune began making plans to be missionaries in Africa. They spent that next year taking training courses on the African diet, socialization process and other important details that would aid them in their four-year stint on another continent.

When they had nearly completed their education and had already been assigned to a village in a remote tribal area, Ralph had an idea. He had been trained in Bible education and knew well the message he and Cheri would present to the tribal people. But he had never studied the power of healing through prayer.

"I think I'm going to take that course," Ralph told his wife one afternoon.

Cheri nodded and shrugged her shoulders. "Why not?"

The two had discussed the course, and Cheri, pregnant with their first child, had decided she would not have time for the additional work. But Ralph was intrigued. If he was going to tell the people about God's love, then he'd better be prepared to tell them about His healing power as well.

Although raised in the Christian church and well-versed on Scripture, Ralph had never thought much of the preachers who did healing demonstrations. Many of them had proved to be frauds over the years. Even worse, a number had been swindlers who only performed trickery in exchange for donations. And so to consider the true healing nature of God was a new idea for Ralph.

He began the class at about the same time that Cheri visited a doctor for what had become a persistent and painful lower and middle-back pain.

"I'm afraid I have bad news for you, Mrs. Brune," the doctor told her as the two sat in his office after her examination. "The X-rays show that you're suffering from the early stages of scoliosis."

The doctor went on to explain that scoliosis was a disease that caused the spine to begin to curve unnaturally, forcing the body to become severely hunched and causing excruciating pain in its victims. When the disease occurs in children, it can be managed with a series of braces, since the child's skeletal frame is still growing. But when it strikes an adult, there is nothing that can be done.

"What can I expect?" Cheri asked, fighting tears. The news was devastating. She and Ralph had so many plans for the future. If she was going to be strong enough to bear children and live the rugged life of a missionary in Africa, she would need a healthy back.

"The pain you're experiencing will get worse. Within the next two years you will be able to notice the curving in your spine. I'm sorry."

Cheri nodded in resignation and returned home to share the news with Ralph.

They talked about it, and then he told her his own news. He had met twice already with the class on healing through prayer. He told her he was impressed with the stories he was hearing. Not stories of tent-revival healings or televised miracles, but quiet stories of health changes that in his opinion could be nothing less than modern-day miracles.

That night as they were falling asleep, Ralph sat up in bed and spoke to Cheri in the dark of their room.

"Would you mind if I pray for your back, Cheri?"

Cheri shrugged, already partially asleep. "Sure. Do I have to move?"

"No. You're fine."

Cheri was lying on her side, a position that favored her painful back. As she lay, falling asleep, Ralph spent thirty minutes holding his hands above her back and praying silently that God would heal her condition.

Each night for a week he continued this routine. Just as they were about to go to sleep, he would sit up, place his hands over Cheri's back, and pray specifically for God to heal her scoliosis. On the seventh night something strange happened.

Ralph had been praying for his wife for ten minutes when suddenly he spoke.

"Cheri?"

"Yes?" She was still awake.

"Do you feel anything?"

"Just your hand moving up and down along my spine."

Ralph's eyes widened in surprise. "Cheri, I haven't touched your back." Ralph shook his head. "I'm serious, Cheri. I haven't touched you. The only reason I asked if you felt something was because I had my hand over your back and at that moment I was feeling something warm passing beneath my hand."

"What do you think it was?"

"I don't know. But I'm going to keep praying."

Cheri yawned and lay back down on their bed. "It can't hurt. Besides, I know God *could* heal me if He wanted to. I just don't know if that's part of His plan for us. Modern miracles and all."

"By the way, how's your pain?" Ralph asked.

Cheri paused a moment and then sat upright once more. "You know, actually I can't feel it."

There was silence between them for a moment as they considered the warmth that had passed along Cheri's back and the feeling of a human hand moving up and down her spine.

"Do you think," Cheri asked quietly, "I might be healed?"

"I think we need to see how you feel tomorrow and in the meantime keep praying."

Two weeks later, after Cheri and Ralph had flown to Portland to visit her parents, she visited a doctor who had known her as a child. She brought with her the X-rays and diagnosis: severe scoliosis, which appeared to be progressing rapidly.

Then, upon Cheri's request, the doctor took another set of X-rays and performed an additional examination of her spine.

"I don't know how to explain this," the doctor said as he reentered the examination room. "Cheri, there's no sign of any scoliosis at all. Your back is perfectly normal."

Cheri was stunned. She remembered the night when she had felt a hand moving gently along her back. "Could it somehow have reversed itself?" she asked the doctor, wanting to be absolutely sure about what had happened.

"No. For a person to have scoliosis as severely as you did in these last X-rays"— the doctor held the photographs up to the light and shook his head—"you definitely would have had scar tissue, even if it has somehow reversed itself."

"Then how do you explain it?"

The doctor put the films gently on a nearby table and smiled at Cheri. "I've learned over the years that there are some things we on Earth cannot explain when it comes to medical healings. I like to call them miracles."

Cheri shared with the doctor the incident weeks earlier when Ralph had been praying and she had felt a hand on her spine at the same time that he felt a warmth passing beneath his hand. To Cheri's surprise, the doctor nodded.

"Yes, when we hear of this type of thing, and we don't hear about it very often, there is often a warmth associated with it. It doesn't take a lot of believing on my part. After all, the human body itself is a working miracle. That our Creator would continue to work miracles within us is, in my opinion, quite possible."

Months later when Cheri and Ralph left for Africa, it was in good health and with a deep respect and belief for the kind of prayer that God answers in the form of miraculous healing.

WHAT GOD HAS DONE

JOAN WESTER ANDERSON

im McNamara of Mokena, Illinois, worked for Sears Roebuck in the Chicago area, and his job involved calling on people in their homes. "I had found the Lord in a big way," Jim says, "so from time to time, I'd witness about Him to customers if they seemed open to it."

One day Jim had an appointment with an older couple, Mr. and Mrs. Sam Lynch, who lived on Chicago's South Side. Their warmth and hospitality were evident, and Jim liked them immediately. "After we concluded our business," Jim recalls, "I noticed a huge Bible lying on their coffee table. 'That's a very important book, isn't it?' I asked the couple."

They both nodded. "It certainly is."

Briefly, Jim told them about how he had come to know Jesus. When he had finished, Louise Lynch nodded to her husband. "Tell him what happened to you, Sam," she said.

"Well," Sam said shyly, "I'm a carpenter. And one day I felt the Lord asking me to build a church for him. And so I did."

"You did? A whole church?" Jim was astounded.

"Well, I subcontracted some of the work. But I did the plans, and most of the labor. It's still open today. The Leclaire Missionary Baptist Church on Lavergne Avenue. My name is even on a piece of the concrete wall." Sam sat back.

But there was more to the story. "Tell him what happened after it was built," Louise prodded.

Sam squirmed in his chair. Apparently, this part was harder to relate. "When they were making plans to dedicate the church, the deacons and people wanted me to read the Bible from the pulpit," Sam explained. "I kept saying no, but they kept asking."

"Why didn't you want to read?" Jim asked.

The Lynches looked at each other. "He couldn't," Louise said softly. "Sam had been illiterate his whole life. In fact, my mother originally forbade me to marry him because he couldn't read. She didn't think he would amount to anything."

The couple eventually wed, but they had always kept Sam's disability a secret. No one had ever known about it except the three Lynch children, who, as they grew, would read to their father from newspapers and books. Sam had a quick mind and a marvelous memory, so no one ever guessed his secret. But now, if people from the congregation kept pressuring Sam, perhaps he would have to admit it. Neither he nor Louise was happy about that.

Eventually Louise came up with a solution. "We'll choose some verses," she told Sam, "and I'll read them over and over to you, and you'll memorize them. Then you can stand up at the pulpit, and it will *look* like you're reading. No one will ever know."

Sam relented. "We practiced pretty hard, every night," he told Jim. "But the verses were short and no one knew what I was planning to read anyway, so I figured I could get through it."

The morning of the dedication came, and the church was full. Louise was sitting in the first row, and she watched proudly as Sam ascended the steps to the pulpit, picked up the Bible and began to read. And then . . . her heart seemed to stop.

For Sam was not reciting the verses they had practiced together. Nor was he repeating anything remotely resembling material he knew or was familiar with. No, instead he was reading—loudly, confidently, even turning pages.

Jim had listened to the story enthralled. "How did the people in the audience react?" he now asked.

"They didn't know anything special was going on," Louise answered. "Since no specific material had been planned, they just assumed Sam was reading what he had selected. He went on and on. I don't think even he fully realized what was happening."

"I didn't," Sam added. "Not until I got home and the whole impossible situation hit me. Then I picked up a book—just to see if it had been some big mistake. And you know what? I could still read."

For the rest of his life Sam read, although sometimes a little slowly. Eventually, he engaged a tutor who came to his house and helped him progress even more. But he and Louise never forgot the marvel of that special day in church.

"God healed the blind man," Jim McNamara says. "He said, 'Lazarus, come out!' And He must have said, 'Sam, read My Scriptures.' What a God we serve!"

WHEN NO ONE ELSE BELIEVED

QUIN SHERRER

As soon as the doctor came into her hospital room, Sandy Horn planned to shake her fists in his face and demand that he tell her the truth about the extent of her malignancy.

The doctor and Sandy's husband, Earl, were huddling out in the hall, deciding how much to tell her. They decided to lay out the facts. When they entered the room, the doctor took the X-rays he had brought and pointed to five malignant spots he had circled. She had cancer in her neck, in the top and bottom left ribs, in her pelvic bone, and at the tip of her spine. When his only prescription was cobalt treatment, the seriousness of his words hit her. She had inoperable cancer.

Sandy was thirty-four years old, bursting with enthusiasm for life and enjoying the gypsy style of moving wherever the space industry transferred Earl. They had three healthy young children, who needed her. She desperately fought the thought of dying so young. She tells her story.

God was my only hope. I was used to taking my problems to Him, and I turned to Him now with specific prayers for healing. I felt so close to Him as I whiled away those lonely afternoons in bed, searching the Scriptures for promises I knew He would reveal.

When I was thirteen, soon after my baptism in a Tennessee mountain stream, I had heard a preacher say that God still heals sick bodies. But my aunt had convinced me that miracles were outdated. Now as I lay on my sick bed afternoon after afternoon, I could not find anything in my Bible telling me miracles were exclusively for first-century Christians.

I began to claim the promise of healing, especially as I read and reread from my old King James Bible the Scripture from James 5:14 that says to call the elders of the church to pray over the sick, anointing them with oil in the name of the Lord, and the prayer of faith would save the sick person. I asked God to send me some elders. I didn't think the elders in my own church would consider such a prayer, but I knew somehow God would work it out. I believed I would be healed even when no one else wanted to talk about it. My husband, Earl, was especially annoyed when I brought up the subject.

Over the next few weeks I underwent thirty-four cobalt treatments—but only in the throat area, where the first cancer had shown up. Doctors would later decide which malignant spot would be treated next. After all, I had five.

I had to make the one-hundred-and-thirty-mile round-trip from my home to the hospital each day. As the weeks stretched out, I realized the importance of time. How I treasured it—time with my family, time spent talking to God.

Some days I had a real battle with self-pity. "It isn't fair," I would wail. "I'm five hundred miles from my mother, and there's nobody to help care for me." Earl had to leave early for his job, so each morning, no matter how I felt, I got Donna and Ricky off to school and took Jim in the car with me—for a sixty-five-mile drive into Hattiesburg, Mississippi.

As the cobalt treatments in my throat progressed, various muscles began to collapse. The doctor said the inside of my throat was starting to look like a raw piece of beef. Yet despite everything, I believed Jesus would heal me.

In the meantime, each night I prayed for strength to make it through the next day. "Just enough, Lord, to make it to the hospital and home again," I would ask.

As I grew weaker, little Jim and I sang Christmas carols so I wouldn't fall asleep while driving. Soon I was depending on my three-year-old son to zip my dress. Eventually friends volunteered to drive me to the hospital each day. How I needed them!

Late one Sunday night, right before Christmas, my pastor and a visiting Taiwanese missionary knocked on our door. Could they pray for me? they asked. Surely they were the elders I had prayed would come!

They prayed specifically that God would heal me. After they left, I stretched out in bed beside Earl. As I began praising God silently, a strange sensation pulsated through my body, much like an ocean wave engulfing me.

I felt a surge of power wash up from my toes, extend to my head and rush back down through my body to my toes again. The power of Jesus had healed my body!

I had met my risen Lord as I had never met Him before.

I nudged my sleeping husband. "I am healed, Earl. I am healed," I said excitedly.

"I'm glad," he mumbled as he fell back into a deep sleep, obviously not taking me seriously.

I sank to my knees beside the bed, praising God and thanking Him for healing me.

In the weeks that followed I shared my belief in my healing with my friends.

"I'm healed," I repeated over and over again.

"That's nice, but don't get your hopes up."

"Jesus healed me," I would tell someone else.

"It's not good for you to get excited," they would answer.

"Earl, I know that Jesus came to me and healed me."

"Sandy, I don't think that kind of talk is too good for you right now."

I waited impatiently for the first week of February, when I was scheduled to go into the hospital for scans to see where they should start the next cobalt treatment. Supposedly, the scans would determine where the malignancy was spreading the fastest. I knew the scan would show I'd been healed.

The day before I was to check into the hospital, I was suddenly frightened. What if everybody else was right and I was wrong? What if God hadn't really healed me and I had only imagined the physical sensation?

That afternoon my daughter came home from a friend's house, carrying a copy of *Guideposts*. In it I read a story of former Army General Bruce Medaris, one-time head of Redstone Arsenal, where my husband worked. The magazine told how he had been divinely healed of cancer. "Of course God is still healing today," I shouted, "and he has healed me too."

I woke the next morning to the tune of soft choir music. I heard each word clearly as voices blended, singing about Jesus, my friend. Jumping out of bed, I found an old church songbook. There I found the words to the song I had just heard, though it had been twenty years since I had last sung it: "There's not a friend like the lowly Jesus—No, not one! No, not one!" Had I heard a heavenly choir? My assurance returned. I had a deep feeling there would be no need for further treatments.

After one day of scans and another day of X-rays, the radiologist gave me the results. "You have won the first round," he said. "Nothing showed up." They ran more tests. Again, no sign of cancer.

Earl and I asked to see both sets of scans—the original ones showing the five malignant spots and the scans just completed. Looking at them, we knew I was home free. Well! Complete! Whole! Healed! "Thank God!" I cried tears of happiness and joy. Earl rushed to telephone our closest friends, not afraid now to tell them, "Sandy's been healed by Jesus."

As I began my last trip home from the hospital, a Bible verse kept running through my mind. "Return home and tell how much God has done for you" (Luke 8:39, NIV).

That was twenty-eight years ago. Earl became a Christian as a result of my healing, and I have had many opportunities to tell others that the supernatural power of God is available for healing today.

BECAUSE HE IS GOOD

Rebekah Montgomery

ate summer 1979, Zanesville, Indiana.

Not many miracles begin with a sneeze; however, Rose Mary Lampton's did.

The summer was drawing to an end, and Rose's children had returned to school. She was enjoying a quiet moment at the breakfast table with her husband when late-summer allergies made her sneeze. Recoiling, discovered that she had injured her back and couldn't straighten up. In a lot of pain but amused at the absurd way in which she had hurt herself, she asked her husband Joe to help her to the living room sofa. Rose had experienced backaches since she was a high-school girl, so she thought if she could rest for a time, her back would right itself.

Rose was scheduled to play piano later that morning at the church, a scant three blocks away. She tried to walk the distance, but the pain became so excruciating that a neighbor had to help her home. Eventually, the pain was so bad that she had to be hospitalized.

Rose could not understand why this backache was so painful and persistent. But the orthopedic surgeon at the small-town hospital pinpointed her problem. "I did the surgery on one of your brothers when he had back problems," he told her. "His slipped disc looks just like yours. You're heading for surgery, just like him."

After a week in the hospital, Rose was released to complete bed rest. Although she attempted to stay off her feet and read books, as a mother who was trying to hold a job at the local post office while caring for her family, Rose could not afford to wile away each day in bed.

"I tried to decide I was well, but I had so much pain by the end of the day, it would be just awful," said Rose. "The pain ran down my right leg and would make my toe numb. Joe was working in the evenings and he would get off at nine, but I'd be so exhausted that I'd be asleep by the time he got home. I would think I was sleeping soundly, but I was tossing and turning and moaning out loud. I was making so much noise, he couldn't get any sleep."

One evening a short while later, her father stopped in to see her. Rose was standing at the sink washing the dishes, and she said to him, "Dad, I know you've prayed for my back before, but would you pray for me one more time?"

Rose's father laid his large, callused hand on her and prayed a prayer she has never forgotten. "God, we ask You to heal her not because we're good, but because You're good."

Said Rose, "I thought I could believe now that God could heal me. My silent prayer was a prayer of faith based on the fact that God was good, not that I was."

When Rose walked her father to the door, she noticed that there wasn't any pain down her leg. "I thought at the time, *Maybe it'll come back*," said Rose. "But I put the kids to bed and went to bed myself and slept soundly."

The next morning, she still felt fine. "I wondered. *Is this really happening?* But I didn't want to say anything until I was sure," Rose said.

After two nights without listening to his wife moan in her sleep, Joe called Rose from work. "What happened to your back? You haven't been tossing and turning at night," he asked.

"I think God healed me," Rose told him.

"I knew something happened because you've been sleeping like a log," he responded.

Rose did not have to have surgery nor have her back problems returned. She still has allergies.

Postscript

Rose Mary Lampton's four older brothers have had to have surgery to repair slipped discs, the same back condition from which she believes she was healed.

Rose still works for the U.S. Post Office, Markle and Fort Wayne, Indiana, offices. Her husband Joe manages a Dollar General store and pastors a United Methodist Church. The Lamptons have three children and three grandchildren and live in Zanesville, Indiana.

"NOT MY WAY BUT YOURS..."

JOAN WESTER ANDERSON

W hen Duane Miller awakened on Sunday morning, January 14, 1990, his throat was raw, his voice a bit raspy. But he barely gave it a thought.

Scheduled to preach two morning services that day, he was already mentally reviewing his material: Would his congregation be consoled, informed, hopefully inspired by his words? As senior pastor of First Baptist Church in Brenham, Texas, Duane loved God, loved to preach and sing (he had started singing professionally at the age of sixteen), and loved family life with his wife, Joylene, and their two college-aged daughters. And although his church was suffering through some financial problems—which often resulted in twenty-hour workdays for Duane—his natural optimism was strong. With God on his side, what could go wrong?

Now, however, as Duane prepared for the day, he experienced that ominous stuffy, headachy, dizzy feeling that usually heralds the flu. Drinking hot tea, he managed to preach at the first service, but singing was all but impossible—even his range seemed limited to just a few notes. "During my second sermon, every sound and inflection grated on the back of my throat like sandpaper," Duane recalls. He cut his talk short, canceled the rest of his duties and reluctantly went home to bed. Obviously the long work hours had finally caught up with him.

The flu took almost ten days to abate. But Duane's throat did not recover. "It was painful and constricted, as if someone had my windpipe between his two fingers and was squeezing it whenever I swallowed," he explains. "There was a constant choking sensation. My voice was weak and hoarse." When Duane finally saw a physician, the throat was so swollen that the doctor could not get a scope down to examine it. Duane's nightmare had begun.

The doctor was almost certain of the diagnosis. He suspected that the flu germ had penetrated the protective sheath around the vocal cords and permanently destroyed them. Duane was probably going to live the rest of his life without a normal voice. But there was the possibility that the doctor's suspicions weren't correct. He wanted Duane to try some medication and visit several specialists.

When, fourteen days later, there seemed to be no real improvement from the medication he had started taking, Duane went to the Baylor College of Medicine in Houston for more tests. On their recommendation, he took a six-month leave of absence from his church, in order to stay home and speak as infrequently as possible. Perhaps his voice—his whole body—was just worn out and needed some time to recover.

Duane was discouraged during this time, but not panic-stricken. After all, he was a man of faith, who believed that God could and often did heal. God was obviously taking His time about answering Duane's prayers, but of course He would answer. Hadn't He called Duane to the ministry, where speaking was absolutely essential? Despite his fears, Duane was willing to wait until God disclosed more of His always-perfect plan.

But God revealed nothing, and as time passed new symptoms developed: Duane lost his equilibrium, and often his vision would blur. Was he going to lose his sight now as well as his voice? Life slowly became unworkable, unbearable. How could one communicate, earn a living, even take care of errands without being able to make the most minimal of sounds? Financial difficulties grew. "The mortgage company, phone company, the grocer—no one gives discounts just because you've lost your voice," Duane says. But surely the answers would come.

They did not. After the leave of absence ended, Duane's voice hadn't improved, and the physicians offered no new alternatives. The original diagnosis had been correct. There was no hope of reversing the situation. Duane could still emit some sounds, but these were produced by fatty tissue near the vocal cords (known as "false cords"), and in time these too would wear away. Within a year or so, the doctors agreed, Duane would be completely mute.

Brokenhearted, Duane officially resigned his pastorate. The family returned to First Baptist Church in Houston, one of the largest church communities in the country, where Duane had served for twelve years prior to going to Brenham, and where they had many old friends. "I faced the indignity of more medical tests, the humiliation of being without a vocational future, the anguish of watching my singing and preaching ministry being completely shut down," Duane writes in his book, *Out of the Silence.* "But I no longer faced them alone." Duane had always been the giver in this congregation; now he was in need. It was not the role he would have chosen, but for a little while, being surrounded by friends made life more bearable.

Joylene and the girls found jobs (which paid the college bills), Duane ran an agency involving work he could do on paper rather than vocally, and the family managed to rent a house they all liked very much. And when several physicians were almost positive that Duane had multiple sclerosis, the final test result was negative. In the midst of the agony, there was always just a trace of hope.

Duane was fully aware that people suffered handicaps and physical pain far more crippling than his. And yet, his voice was essential to the job he had always *assumed* God had called him to do. What had changed? Did God now find him unworthy?

"The anguish of my physical impairment began to bludgeon my spiritual life as well," Duane recalls. "If I hear anyone who goes through a trying test say he or she never doubted God, I think that person is either lying or has lost touch with reality."

What are You doing, God? Don't You love me anymore? Have You abandoned me? How many people throughout history, both famous and obscure, have struggled with these questions? Duane Miller was no exception.

By now, because his condition was so rare, Duane had become a medical celebrity. At one seminar in Switzerland, specialists from all over the world examined photos of his throat. "From the very beginning, everything had been recorded and documented, like time-lapse photography," he explains, "because every time I went to see any doctor, he would put the scope down my throat and photograph the changes, especially the growing scar tissue."

It was as if God wanted everything officially recorded—wanted everyone to see that the glory, when it came, would be all His.

During these agonizing years, Duane learned to make himself heard by using a sort of guttural pressure, forcing air through his throat and "screaming" at the top of his lungs. Finally someone from the congregation found a microphone that, when pressed against Duane's lips, could amplify these sounds, which opened up a new possibility: Perhaps Duane could occasionally teach his former Sunday school class at First Baptist. He was hesitant. Who would want to listen to such uncomfortable sounds? But his friends encouraged him, and once in a while he preached a short lesson.

He was doing just that on the morning of January 17, 1993, having been persuaded to substitute at the last minute for another teacher. The class was also being tape-recorded, a routine practice. The two hundred or so attendees knew about Duane's voice. But because Duane had always tried to keep the more personal problems to himself, no one in the audience was aware that he had recently lost his job and his medical insurance; had had a book proposal rejected (not because of his writing ability but because he would not be physically able to do any media promotion); or that he was nearing the time when the doctors believed he would become completely mute—in short, that he was as low as he had been since the beginning of his ordeal. Nor had Duane selected that particular day's lesson, based on Psalm 103, since the series had been scheduled seven years in advance. "I was feeling no great faith—in fact, inside, I was still asking God, *Why have You punished me this way?*" Duane recalls.

In Psalm 103:3–5 (NIV), God reminds us not to forget:

> *who forgives all your sins*
> *and heals all your diseases,*
> *who redeems your life from the pit . . . .*
> *so that your youth is renewed like the eagle's.*

These were hard concepts for Duane to discuss. He truly believed that God does such things. But everyone in the congregation had watched Duane struggle for three years; they knew that God had not healed or renewed their beloved friend, despite his courage and goodness. How effective a teaching could this be?

Duane spoke for more than twenty minutes before reaching these particular verses, and he was just about ready to cut the lesson short—his throat was hurting terribly. The strain of pushing the words out was so great that he wondered if anyone could hear him anyway. "I have had, and you've had, pit experiences," he forged on. Pit experiences . . . that's where he was now, in a pit with no way out . . . . Suddenly, on the word *pit*, Duane felt something odd. The "hands" that had been locking his throat for three years seemed to let go! People looked up—what had happened? Duane sounded different.

Duane noticed it too. His voice was stronger, less hoarse. "Now . . . to say God doesn't do miracles today is to put God in a box, and God doesn't like to be put in a box," he said. Then he stopped, stunned. He could hear himself! His voice was normal.

Joylene left her chair in the audience and ran up to the stage. "I don't . . . understand this right now," Duane said without the microphone. "In fact, I'm at a loss for words!" He put his arms around Joylene and began to weep. Some in the congregation broke into tears, some cheered, laughed, and praised God.

Others dashed out of the room to find the senior pastor. "Duane's been healed!" they shouted.

Could it be true? "I wanted to laugh, cry, sing, shout, dance, and hug everyone I could, all at the same time," Duane recalls. "After a few brief minutes, I thought, What better way to celebrate the restoration of my voice than to teach God's word?" So he continued the lesson. And at the end of the session, the congregation burst into the most appropriate of all endings, the doxology: *Praise God from Whom all blessings flow* . . . "I don't think anyone who was there that day will ever sing the doxology in a casual manner again," Duane says. "The truth of its simplicity struck our hearts for eternity."

Word, of course, had started to spread. Dr. John Bisagno, senior pastor of the church, was conducting the scheduled worship service in the main church and now summoned Duane to the platform. People who had attended the early service had heard about Duane's restored voice, so now there was standing room only in the worship center as Dr. Bisagno began. "He's been around here for the best part of twenty years. And most of you know the problem he has had with his voice these past three years. I want him to come and tell you what God has done in his life."

Duane approached the pulpit. "Well, I'll try," he said. At that, some five thousand people jumped to their feet and began to worship God much as Duane's earlier class had done. Some wept, some laughed, others clapped; many fell to their knees and their tears flowed freely. The organist began to play the Bill Gaither chorus, "Let's Just Praise the Lord!" And everyone did.

Since his healing, Duane has been back to many physicians for reevaluation, and every photo taken of his throat since January 17, 1993, shows a complete lack of scar tissue on his vocal cords. They are as smooth and as healthy as they were before his tribulation began, with absolutely no indication that any problem ever existed.

"Even if you could explain the coincidence of my suddenly being able to speak," Duane says, "you have to understand that scar tissue doesn't disappear by itself. What happened to it?"

And yet, after much thought, Duane is convinced that this is the central message of his entire experience. Scar tissue—at least the spiritual kind—does disappear. God has said that He will perform glorious works for His children, and what could be more glorious than knowing that our lives, with all their failures and mistakes, can be completely restored in an instant, through His love and grace?

Nor should the very public aspect of Duane's miracle be overlooked. Not only did the witnesses in his congregation and throughout Houston experience a deepening of their faith, but word spread throughout the world, primarily because the entire event had been tape-recorded. So often miracles are private, tender in their intimacy. But in this case, God had unleashed the tongues of thousands, all eager to share the good news. Ironically, Duane himself is one of them, now a radio talk show host each day on KKHT in Houston—when he's not on the road preaching what he believes to be an important lesson to audiences in every part of the country. "God healed me, not because I earned it, deserved it, had enough people praying, or any of those other reasons," Duane says, "but because He wanted people to be drawn to Him and to give Him all the glory."

Many believe that this is just the beginning of the glory God is going to reveal to His people in the coming years. Our God—yours, mine, and Duane's—is truly an awesome God.

Series Editor: Patricia S. Klein
Designed by Monica Elias
Jacket photo courtesy of Photodisc
Typeset by Composition Technologies, Inc.
Printed in the United States of America

This original Guideposts book was created by the Book and Inspirational Media Division of the company that publishes *Guideposts*, a monthly magazine filled with true stories of people's adventures in faith.

Guideposts is available by subscription. All you have to do is write to Guideposts, 39 Seminary Hill Road, Carmel, New York 10512. When you subscribe, each month you can count on receiving exciting new evidence of God's presence, His guidance and His limitless love for all of us.

Guideposts is also available on the Internet by accessing our home page on the World Wide Web at www.guideposts.org. Send prayer requests to our Monday morning Prayer Fellowship. Read stories from recent issues of our magazines, *Guideposts, Angels on Earth, Guideposts for Kids,* and *Guideposts for Teens,* and follow our popular book of devotionals, *Daily Guideposts.* Excerpts from some of our best-selling books are also available.